The Adam and Eve agenda

*For David and Joyce in gratitude
for years of love and support.*

THE
ADAM AND EVE
AGENDA

Male and female
– who's in charge?

Derek Wood

Inter-Varsity Press

INTER-VARSITY PRESS
38 De Montfort Street, Leicester LE1 7GP, England

Unless otherwise stated, Scripture
quotations in this publication are from
the Holy Bible, New International Version.
Copyright © 1973, 1978, 1984 International
Bible Society. Published in Great Britain
by Hodder and Stoughton Ltd.

First published 1992

British Library Cataloguing in Publication Data
A catalogue record for this book is available from the British Library.

ISBN 0-85110-865-2

Set in 11/12.5pt Clearface
Typeset in Great Britain by Saxon Printing Ltd, Derby

Printed in Great Britain by Cox & Wyman Ltd, Reading, Berks

Inter-Varsity Press is the book-publishing division of the Universities and Colleges Christian Fellowship (formerly the Inter-Varsity Fellowship), a student movement linking Christian Unions in universities and colleges throughout the United Kingdom and the Republic of Ireland, and a member movement of the International Fellowship of Evangelical Students. For information about local and national activities write to UCCF, 38 De Montfort Street, Leicester LE1 7GP.

Contents

Foreword

Every once in a while you come across a book that is a bit special. We felt that way a few years ago when a friend gave us a copy of Derek Wood's book *The Barnabas Factor*. It may have had something to do with the fact that Barnabas is one of our favourite Bible characters – we have long regarded him as an unsung hero of the New Testament Church. But we were intrigued to meet the characters of Canwell Park, who brought to life the way in which the lost ministry of encouragement can be recovered by Christians working through the up-and-down realities of life in a local church.

We have followed with interest the books that followed in the series, *The Simon Peter File* and *The Jacob Portfolio*, with the Canwell Park crowd developing as a religious mixture of *The Archers* and *East-Enders*. Derek Wood has a rare ability to weave biblical truth into 'an everyday story of Christian folk'.

This book is the fourth (and last) in the Canwell Park series. It tackles the thorny issue of what has been described as 'the battle of the sexes'. What does the Bible teach about the role and status of men and women? Does headship simply mean male dictatorship? How can we interpret the Bible in a modern world? Are we guilty of reading it through our own cultural spectacles?

It is a brave person who sets out to address these questions which are (sadly) points of division for many Christians.

Derek Wood doesn't pretend to provide all the answers, but through the eyes of the Canwell Park congregation he helps us to see the direction in which the answers lie.

We came away from reading this book with three convictions. First, the Bible *does* have something valid to say about the roles men and women have to play in the world, the church and the home. Second, that we need to learn to think and act 'Christianly' in our dealings with each other. And third, that to interpret the Bible's message in any culture means that there are principles to be followed and prejudice to be avoided.

The Adam and Eve Agenda is a book to get people thinking, listening and talking – preferably in that order!

Ian and Ruth Coffey

1

A picnic

Gordon Barber firmly closed his eyes. The bank he was lying on was not comfortable. A tussock of grass had forced its way into the small of his back. He realized how hot it was. Very hot for early September. Thundery. A fly was walking across his face. He waved it away and closed his eyes again. The fly walked across his bald head.

Gordon's wife Margaret looked across at her husband and sighed. He was looking old. How old was he? Funny how you lose count. Thirty-five; two years older than she was. He worked too hard, that was the trouble. He had a responsible job as a senior accountant with Drew, Drew & Drew in the City and he came home to the same kind of work again as church treasurer.

It wasn't just a question of counting the Sunday collections. The church had embarked on an ambitious programme of rebuilding which was to cost well over £300,000. There had been much controversy and some members were still not happy with the project. They were well short of the target and Gordon tended to take too much responsibility for it all.

Shelley was a handful too. Shelley was their only child. She was a delight in many ways, bright and attractive but strong-willed and single-minded. For two long and noisy years her single mind had been dominated by pop music. Gordon and Margaret shared a great love for Palestrina and Byrd, so that the generation between them and Shelley seemed to be stretched to four centuries when music was mentioned. Which was often.

Just now Shelley was trying to play with Rebecca. Rebecca was six months old and by no means ready to play with anybody. Margaret's wifely concern for Gordon turned to motherly concern for Shelley, or rather Rebecca and her mother, Diana. She sighed again and put down her book. Why was it that she could never get properly involved with a book without having to worry about Gordon (he's working his way towards a heart-attack, or at least a stomach ulcer) or Shelley (what *is* that child doing now?) or all the other troubled people who seemed to need her listening ear and wise counsel? It was a privilege to be needed, certainly, but just this once surely she could have a few minutes' peace?

'Shelley dear, don't bother the baby. She needs a sleep,' said Margaret.

'So do we all,' growled Gordon, waving away the fly.

'No. Rebecca told me she wants to play with me.' Shelley's eyes challenged her mother's.

'Shelley Barber. You are nine. You know quite well that babies of six months old do not speak.'

'Oh, we speak soul to soul,' said Shelley dreamily, opening her brown eyes very wide.

Diana's serious face exploded with laughter and Margaret had to admit that she'd lost another verbal duel with Shelley. Having won her point Shelley moved away at a dignified pace.

Peace was restored. Gordon settled down once more with his fly, Margaret with her book, and Diana Monteith looked down with adoring eyes on her baby daughter.

Cheerfully determined

The occasion was a 'Vicar's voyage'. The church council at St Barnabas' made a habit of organizing an occasional picnic on a Saturday when a few members and their families took Timothy and his wife Diana on an outing to ensure that they had some time off. Timothy wondered whether a picnic on a stuffy September day with some of his church members was really a holiday or an extension of the church council, but they meant well and he didn't like to refuse the offer.

Just now he and the other four 'voyagers' had left the Barbers with Diana and baby Rebecca and were toiling up a bracken-clad hillside, all five dripping with perspiration. The sky in front of them looked decidedly grey, but everyone seemed cheerfully determined to reach the top and get back to base before the rain came.

Timothy, bringing up the rear, found himself wondering how the two couples in front of him were going to manage their new lives. Two recently-married couples. In fact Bob and Gina had been married only a few weeks.

He looked at them again. Bob was holding Gina's hand with noble determination, even though the path among the bracken was almost non-existent and he was having to force his way through the undergrowth. Typical Bob, thought Timothy. A man of strong will but limited imagination, marrying for the first time at 53 and very anxious to make a success of it.

His wife, Gina, now clad in khaki shorts and walking boots, was also a strong character. A widow of six years, she had survived serious depression, experienced remarkable healing and spiritual renewal and was a leading light in church activities. She and Bob had agonized deeply about whether they should marry. Gina had a university degree and now held a senior post in the Council offices at Canford Heath. Bob had a responsible job too, in the safety department of London Underground, but he lacked both his wife's education and her spiritual maturity. After a long and difficult decision-making process, in which Timothy and Diana and Gordon and Margaret had been exhaustingly involved, Gina had said 'yes', Bob had sold his flat and they had set up home in Gina's semi-detached house in Fairview Avenue.

They seemed to be managing so far. Gina was more subdued than usual, but it must have been very hard to welcome another man into the home where she and Andrew had been so happy. Then, thought Timothy, they had used the old-fashioned form of the vow in the

12

marriage service. Gina had promised to obey. That was unusual these days. They had both said they wanted it that way. But it could create problems for those two.

Now Bob had grown a beard. Nothing significant in that, perhaps. But Gina was rather non-committal about it. Timothy thought that she didn't really like it. Bob seemed to be trying to say something by growing that beard.

Who does the ironing?

He glanced beyond Gina and Bob to Nigel and Sallie. It was easy to glance at Sallie. Her long brown legs showed to great advantage. Those scanty shorts suited her very well. Her mass of honey-coloured hair bounced a little on her slender shoulders... Timothy looked away and firmly remembered Diana and the baby.

They made a handsome couple, Nigel and Sallie, and they had quite a story to tell. They'd been married almost a year now. Nigel had become a Christian just before the wedding and Sallie soon afterwards. They were involved with house groups and other church activities and seemed to be growing fast in the faith. That faith had cost them both status and wealth, because Nigel had been dismissed from the City finance firm of Crieff-Farbsteen, ostensibly because his department was being reorganized, but basically because he was too honest for the firm to risk having him about.

Since that time, a year ago, he had been out of work. Both Nigel's and Sallie's parents were well off, but were refusing to help because of the disgrace brought upon them by Nigel's speech at the wedding reception. He had announced to everyone that he was now a Christian and that he had lost his job. He had also lost his BMW. With great sadness they had sold their new town house in Canwell Gardens and bought a bungalow in Canford Crescent. Sallie had sold her TR7 and they now shared a second-hand Montego. Sallie's income from Drew, Drew & Drew (she was a junior colleague of Gordon's) was enough to keep them. Just.

They were coming through all these difficulties very well, thought Timothy. If only Nigel could get a job everything would be fine. It didn't seem right that he should be doing the housework and the ironing and the gardening (there wasn't much of that) while Sallie earned the income. Perhaps Timothy was old-fashioned...

A heavy rumble of thunder made him grateful to see that they were near the top and would soon have an excuse to turn back.

Meanwhile Nigel and Sallie were moving ahead of the others.

'It's amazing when you see things from the other side,' Sallie was saying. 'Do you remember how awful it was when we first went to church? How stuffy it all seemed?'

'Yes, and how old-fashioned we thought their ideas on marriage were.'

'Well, they are old-fashioned,' said Sallie, 'as old as the book of Genesis, Timothy says. But perhaps they're right.'

'Yes. I can see that marriage is right,' said Nigel. 'Till death us do part and all that. But this business of who's in charge and who does what is another ballgame. They don't say much, but some of the older people think that

I'm a wimp for not having a job and especially doing the housework. They think a macho chap like me ought to be out there where the action is and you, Sallie my dear, ought to be posing prettily... in front of the sink.'

'Well, perhaps we shall get some ideas from next month's house group,' said Sallie. 'There's a load of stuff about the Garden of Eden. Adam and Eve and how it all ought to be. That should help us, anyway.'

'Sure,' said Nigel doubtfully, 'but it won't tell us who should do the ironing. They didn't do much ironing, did they? I thought that we should be able to see how these other people do it – they've all been Christians for years – and copy them. But they're all different. Bob seems to be doing his best to subdue Gina, if that's possible; Diana seems to have got her knife into poor old Timothy since the baby was born, and dear old Gordon and Margaret are doing a great job, but they're too worn out to have much of a relationship at all. Which of those are we supposed to imitate? Gosh. Look at *that*!'

Nigel's survey of the state of Canwell Park's marriages came to an abrupt halt as they reached the top of the hill at last and found themselves gazing into a dark purple pit of sky. Even as the others joined them the scene was bisected by a brilliant, jagged river of light. They all turned and fled.

Goodwill and rainwater

Meanwhile, back at base, there was a deep silence, broken only by the occasional roll of thunder in the distance. Gordon was asleep. The fly had tired of tormenting him now he was unconscious and had found shelter from the coming storm. Rebecca was asleep too in her cot, while Margaret and Diana were both happily absorbed in their reading.

At that point two things happened at once. Shelley, who had been suspiciously quiet for some time, had crept through the trees carrying a jam jar half-full of water. With enormous relish she poured its contents on to her father's head with the words, 'I baptize you ...'

At the same time heavy drops of rain began to fall on last year's leaves with the sound of tiny pistol-shots. The rain quickly ended the confusion as everyone hastily gathered the remains of the picnic, the rugs, books and baby and bundled them into the two cars.

Breathless and damp, they surveyed the curtain of water that was now drawn around them.

'Those stupid people will be *drowned*,' said Gordon. 'I told them not to go.'

'Oh, I think they'd enjoy the adventure,' said Margaret. 'Love's young dream can survive a wetting.'

'What has Timothy done to deserve this?' pursued Gordon. 'It's supposed to be his day out.'

A few minutes later five bedraggled figures appeared through the downpour, hair plastered to their heads and clothes clinging to their bodies. But their faces were glistening and, as they came within earshot, they all sang in unison,

'Your mercy flows upon us like a river
Your mercy stands unshakeable and true...'

'Oh, look out,' said Gordon, 'here comes the *Sound of Living Waters* brigade.'

'That one isn't in *Sound of Living Waters*,' said Shelley, 'it's from *Spring Harvest*.'

At which point they were all swamped with goodwill and rainwater.

2

A death

'**I**t's not quite as straightforward as it seems,' said Gina. Bob eyed her warily over his coffee cup. 'It won't all fit if you don't interpret it properly.'

'Here we go again,' said Bob, putting down his cup, 'I thought this afternoon was too good to be true. We agreed too easily.'

'This afternoon' had been a week after the washed-out picnic. Gina's cousin, Olga Crisp, had spent the afternoon and early evening with the Renshaws. Olga Crisp was like her cousin, only more so. She was five years older than Gina, was bony and angular and had a crop of short, curly white hair.

Olga had never married and was more than a little

interested in feminist movements. She attended a church where the Bible was not in vogue and which encouraged its members to view Holy Writ as helpful, provided that you didn't take it too seriously, and true enough for the times in which it was written, which were riddled with superstition, dictatorship and male domination.

The apostle Paul was a target of their alternate mirth and ridicule. They represented him as a woman-hating, bigoted, waspish little man with no sense of humour.

Gina and Bob both had a deep respect for the writings of Paul, as they had for the whole of the Bible, and were trying to base their new marriage on the principles of obedience and love described by Paul in his letter to Ephesus. Olga had been at the wedding and Olga had been quick to notice that Gina had promised to obey Bob. Red rags waved in front of a bull would act as a mild sedative compared to a woman promising to obey a man in the presence of Olga Crisp.

So Gina and Bob had been battered by broadside after broadside of contempt, derision and sarcasm. Why ever did they want to put the clock back to the ark? Olga had wanted to know. Bob's mild query as to whether they had clocks in the ark was ignored. Why didn't Bob go the whole hog and drag her about by the hair? Had Gina no respect for womanhood at all?

'I don't know how she keeps it up,' Bob had whispered in a brief lull while Olga had retired, as she put it, 'to powder her nose'.

'To reload her nostrils with gunpowder,' said Bob morosely.

'She's always been like this,' said Gina. 'What worries me is *why* she has to do it. Deep down there's a terrible uncertainty, you know. She's getting louder and louder, trying to cover up her doubts.'

There was no time for more analysis before Olga had returned and Gina had excused herself to put the kettle on. This had provoked another outburst. Why Gina? Couldn't Bob get the tea? Was he lord of the home while Gina was slave of the kitchen? Gina had explained gently that Bob had cooked for himself for thirty years and was really quite an expert, but that this had been her kitchen for the past twenty years and it was her kettle and she was quite used to switching it on without feeling enslaved.

So it had gone on, and Gina and Bob had taken it all quietly and politely, supporting one another at every turn and giving no ground in their defence of the Bible as inspired and trustworthy. They had quietly allowed themselves to be described as 'obscurantists', 'fundamentalists', 'literalists' and once 'evangelicals', a word which Olga delivered as if it were the deepest insult at her command.

Now Olga had gone back to Woking, leaving behind an atmosphere akin to that on a small country railway station after the InterCity 125 has thundered past at full speed.

The cracks appear

'It's not quite as straightforward as it seems,' said Gina.

'But this afternoon...,' Bob began again.

'This afternoon we were united against the common enemy,' said Gina, 'though I dislike calling my relations enemies. We both believe that the Bible is as relevant to life as it is today as for when it was written. That was the point this afternoon. But now she's gone I have to say that it needs to be interpreted before we can apply it.'

'This is the problem.' Bob stirred his coffee too many times. 'I have been brought up to believe the Bible. My mum and dad weren't scholars but they had a deep faith. And they took the Bible literally. I always remember when my old dad said to me, "You'll find a lot of clever-clever people in this world, son, who will try to shake your belief in the Word of God. Don't listen to 'em. They'll say, 'we can believe this bit and not that bit.' They'll say, 'you've got to understand what's behind it.' Don't listen. It's the thin end of the wedge. If you leave out one bit where does it all end? You leave out the lot. It's all or nothing, my lad, and I hope it will be all with you." There was a tear running down his cheek when he said that. It made a deep impression on me.'

Gina put her arm round Bob's shoulder. 'He was right, your dad. It's not up to us to pick and choose what we want to believe. But the principles in the Bible have to be applied to every new age. You can't use them neat like, like...' Gina struggled for a parallel, but Bob got there first.

'That's it. Dilute it. Don't let its full force come at us.'

'I didn't mean that. Look at the example we've got stuck on, husband and wife and headship. The principles in the Bible will always be true, but the conditions change and they have to be re-applied.'

'The principles are obvious,' said Bob. 'God made man. First. Then he made woman *to be a helper for man*. That's in Genesis. And Paul says, "wives, obey your husbands" and, *and*,' he waved away Gina's spluttering protest, 'there's nothing in the Bible that

20

cancels those two statements. And there's nothing that's happened in the world since then to change them. That's clear and straight, no fancy arguments. Now it's time for bed, Mrs Renshaw. We'll talk about it again another time.'

Gina opened her mouth and shut it again. Yes, perhaps another time.

'Is that the emergency?'

As he drew the bedroom curtains Bob noticed the light in the upstairs window of number 64.

'Mrs Goodrich is up late tonight,' he said. 'Perhaps she's going to keep an eye on us to see that we don't argue too much.'

Mrs Goodrich was ninety-seven and had been in bed as long as anyone could remember, especially her daughter Jane, who struggled to look after the old lady. Mrs Goodrich also had a reputation as an observer of human nature and as a reporter of its failings by telephone to her friends in the district. Mrs Goodrich was not a favourite with Gina.

'Oh, don't worry about the old busybody,' she said yawning. 'She can't bother us.'

'No, perhaps you're right.' He turned off the light and was asleep within minutes. Almost at once, it seemed, Bob was dreaming.

In fact he was having a nightmare. He was inside a kind of medieval treadmill. He and several other men were forcing round a huge wooden wheel by walking inside it. They were driving a great hammer, also made of wood, which was thumping, thumping, thumping. This was bad enough, but he had become conscious

21

that the slave-drivers who were urging him on to greater efforts were female. It was all upside down. Women were giving orders to men. And there was nothing he could do about it. Thump, thump, thump...

'There's someone at the door.' Gina was sitting up in bed and reaching for the light. 'It's half-past *three*. Whoever can it be?'

'I'll go,' said Bob, relieved at least that his nightmare was over.

'Be careful, Bob.'

'Well, it's not a burglar. They don't usually knock at the front door.'

Bob was back after a muffled conversation downstairs.

'It's Jane,' he said curtly. 'Her mother's not well. She's panicking. I'll see to it.'

Gina was already out of bed. 'Don't be silly Bob, you can't.'

'I said,' said Bob very slowly and impressively, 'I'll see to it. Get back to bed, Gina.'

Gina wavered for a moment and then very reluctantly returned to bed.

'OK, have it your own way,' she muttered.

Jane was certainly in a state of confusion. She looked much older than her sixty-five years; white hair tumbling about her face, an old raincoat flung over her nightdress. She suffered from arthritis and was moving with difficulty. In addition she was shivering violently from cold or shock or both.

'It's OK, Jane,' Gina heard Bob saying, 'there's nothing to worry about now.'

'But Mother's gone so strange,' said Jane. 'She's horribly pale, almost like a ghost.'

22

The front door clicked shut and Gina could hear nothing more than a receding murmur. She prayed earnestly that Bob really would know what to do.

A few minutes later he was standing at the bedroom door.

'Gina,' he said in a small voice. 'She wants you to come. I think Mrs Goodrich is dead.'

They found Jane, sobbing at the foot of her mother's bed.

'Bob,' said Gina crisply, having taken in the situation in a few seconds, 'go downstairs, put the kettle on and get a pot of tea going – and while it's boiling telephone the emergency doctor. And while you're about it you'd better phone Timothy as well.'

'We can tell Timothy in the morning, love,' said Bob uneasily, 'and wouldn't it be better to dial 999?'

Gina was hoisting Jane on to an armchair and wiping away her tears with a handkerchief. She looked up at her husband who stood wretchedly in the doorway. She said nothing, but her look was quite sufficient to send him scurrying downstairs.

'Hello. Is that the emergency...? Yes. I'm phoning from Mrs Goodrich's house, 64 Fairview Avenue. Yes. We need some advice. I think Mrs Goodrich is dead.'

Two hours later, when Jane had been settled in their spare bedroom, Gina and Bob climbed wearily back to bed. Bob was predictably feeling very foolish.

'I am sorry, Gina love,' he said. 'I don't know what made me think I could do it all like that.'

'Never mind,' said Gina. 'I know what happened. You just took the theory too far. There are limitations to the "man in charge, woman the helper" idea and this was one of them. I think we'll find that there may be others too, but I'd rather not discuss them now or we'll have to get up again before we've got to bed.'

Bob didn't argue.

Is it true that the Bible must be taken as it stands and never 'translated' to meet modern circumstances?

If it should be applied specifically today, how can we know how to do it?

If in doubt read on.

3

First principles

The autumn programme for house groups in Canwell Park was about to begin. Ten or a dozen groups were to meet fortnightly in homes around the district, under the leadership of senior church members. The series this time was to be launched at a general meeting in the church hall at which Timothy, the vicar, proposed to set out some guide-lines and to introduce the subject.

'Male and female, who's in charge?' was the provocative title for the series, though it was admitted from the start that the spotlight would be on the relationship between husband and wife. Timothy urged the hundred or so members present not to try to read arguments for or against having women as prime ministers from the Bible, when the passages chosen for discussion were about home life and marriage or church organization.

Before dividing the meeting into its twelve constitu-ent parts, Timothy offered some general principles for interpreting the Bible. Bob and Gina looked quickly at one another as he began.

'As you know,' said Timothy, 'we are to begin at the beginning, with the early chapters of the book of Genesis. Now please let's avoid arguments about whether it has to be taken as history or as a sort of parable.' Bob and Gina exchanged glances again. 'If we spend time trying to agree as to whether Adam and Eve were two specific people, or were characters in a story and represent the truth about humankind in that way, we shall miss the point of these studies, and probably all finish up with black eyes.

'We have to tackle this question because so many people get worried about it and because a lot of the Bible's teaching is based on the principles that emerge in the early chapters of Genesis.

'Let's put it this way: many of you will hold that these early chapters of Genesis are history. If cameras had been invented, then we could, in theory, see what happened again and again as we played back the video. Well and good. But if these chapters are historical they are like all Bible history – they are recorded so that we may learn the *truths* that they are intending to convey. The facts of Bible history are recorded so that we may learn the truth.

'Now others of you will take Genesis 1-3 as an allegory or parable. Well and good again. But if these chapters are parables, then, like the parables of Jesus, they are told not simply as a good story but to teach *truths*. Jesus said that people who listened to his stories but didn't do anything about them were building houses on sand. So, if Genesis 1-3 is an extended parable, what matters is whether we act on the truths it contains.

'So, either way, we are concerned to understand the message of these chapters and apply it. The question of whether they are history or parable is a fascinating one, but is a red herring as far as the subject of the relationship of male and female is concerned.

'We shall take these chapters, then, as revealing what God wants us to know about the creation of humankind and about his intentions for the relating of man and woman.'

How should we approach the Bible?

A loud buzz of conversation greeted this. Some people thought that Timothy had made a profound statement, some thought he was trying to have his cake and eat it as well, while others were, by this time, thoroughly confused.

'Let us all unite on one point,' resumed Timothy loudly as the buzz subsided. 'What is in the Bible is there because God meant it to be there. It was written by men, no women as far as we know, and shows all manner of human characteristics, but it has proved, down the ages, to be utterly trustworthy in showing people how to live. Properly interpreted it still gives us that guidance today. So how should we approach it?

'We have to recognize that the writers were expressing the truth *as God sees it* into the life situation *as the author saw it*. It was true for them in principle as it is equally true for us. But the details have changed, everyday expressions are different. God said to Moses at the burning bush, "Take off your shoes. This place is holy." To our grandparents he would have said, "Take off your *hat*." Now most of us don't wear hats. Perhaps he would say, "Bow your head". You see what I mean. "Take off your shoes" has a deeper meaning than literally "take your shoes and socks off". It means, "show by your actions that you realize you are in God's presence and worship him."

'So, pens and notebooks ready, here are the four basic rules:

1. *Ask yourself what the passage actually meant when it was written*. Take it at its face value. Make sure you don't read into it your own ideas of what it ought to say. For instance, you may be a teetotaller, but don't try to pretend that Jesus turned water into blackcurrant juice at the wedding in Cana. Stick to what it actually *says*.

2. *Ask yourself, what is the principle behind what was written?* This is where it's easy to go wrong. To take the example of the water into wine again. It would be uncharacteristic of God to show us this miracle as a sign that he will always be relied upon to rescue us from mismanagement. No, he is saying, "I am Lord of every circumstance. Trust in me and see what will happen. Life will turn from being insipid to being rich."

3. *Ask yourself how the principle applies to your life today*. In what ways can we put ourselves at God's

disposal? Be specific, honest and open.

4. (The other three are valueless without this): *What am I going to do about it?* And when I look back after a week or so, *what have I done about it?*

If you follow those simple questions I believe your Bible study will really come alive. Ask God the Holy Spirit to come alongside you and help you (look at John 16:13) and use a Bible commentary or dictionary to help you with question one if you need to.

'Now let's divide into our groups around the leaders and have a go at the first two questions on your sheets.'

Apparent chaos ensued for five minutes or so, but when order was restored, twelve circles of people were hard at work.

No distinction

Gordon Barber was in early trouble with his group. It included Connie Bassett, a huge lady who had spent a lifetime entertaining, as she put it, 'in the halls'. With her loud cockney voice and forthright opinions she had brought new richness to St Barnabas' when she had announced, in public, her conversion two years ago. She was now, for the moment, confused.

''Ow could both of 'em look like God? It says "in the image of God he created them".'

'It doesn't just mean that Adam and Eve *looked* like God,' said Gordon patiently. 'It means that they had some of the characteristics of God.'

'Yer what?' said Connie loudly.

'What do people think this "image of God" means?

It's there in Genesis 1:26-27. God decided to make mankind to be like him and he made them male and female. In what ways are people like God?'

There was a long silence.

'Loving?' suggested someone hopefully.

'Yes, sometimes, not always,' said Gordon.

'Creative?'

'Yes.'

'Clever.'

'Yes, but what does verse 26 say? "Let them rule over the animals." They were to be *responsible* for the world that God had put them in and later we find that they were morally responsible as well – they could choose between right and wrong and had to answer for their choices. Animals don't seem to have that moral sense, do they...'

There was a chorus of protest at this. Almost every member of the group could give an example of a dog or a cat (one lady said a lizard) that knew when it had done wrong and showed its repentance in some way.

When the hubbub died down Gordon explained that he meant that the animals lived by instinct. Many of them killed 'by nature'. We couldn't blame them for their 'wrongdoing'. But men and women 'ought to know better'. That was what he meant by moral responsibility.

'Then come back to the idea of love that Frances mentioned earlier. God is love and it looks as if perfect love is that between Father, Son and Holy Spirit. But he made us capable of love, too, unlike the animals.' As soon as he said this he realized his mistake.

'Star loves me and you can't say he doesn't.' The speaker was a member of the youth fellowship named

Stephanie, whose horse was her constant companion.

'Yes, of course,' said Gordon, 'but you must admit that your love for your mother is deeper and has more variety than your horse's love for you.'

'No,' said Stephanie firmly.

'Well it ought to be,' said Gordon. 'But the main point here is that whatever ways we have of reflecting what God is like, according to Genesis one there is no distinction at all. Men and women are exactly alike.'

'Go *on!*' said Connie with a deep chuckle.

'You know what I mean,' said Gordon. 'They are equally like God and equally unlike God. Men and women are exactly equal as human beings, equally responsible for their actions and equally capable of love. There's no way of claiming here that men are superior to women or women to men. That's what they call nowadays the bottom line.'

Different roles

The second question was causing more trouble than the first. Gina Renshaw was leading a group (Bob had asked to join another one) and was trying to get them to decide what was the principle behind Genesis 2:18-25, the story of the creation of the woman, from the side, or rib, of the man.

One or two people had been sceptical about such a 'far-fetched idea', as they put it, having any principles of truth in it at all. Someone else had quoted the old saying that woman was taken not from man's head to rule over him, nor from his feet to be his slave, but from his side to love him and be next to his heart. This had produced general approval and two pocket handkerchiefs.

'The obvious meaning', said Edith Kent, 'is that Adam needed a helper, someone to keep him company. It says in verse 18 that it's not good for man to be alone.'

'So that means that men take the glory and women mend the socks.' The speaker was Sallie Rogers. 'Doesn't this verse give men the handle they've always needed to keep women in subjection? "I'll do it all, dear, you can help if you like." It's *very* condescending. I suppose it reflects the state of affairs when Genesis was written. But what's the principle for today?'

'Exactly what I was asking,' said Gina. 'At its face value it does look like you say. But one thing we women can thank theologians for is for telling us the meaning and the use of words. And it appears that this word "helper" often appears in the Old Testament and nearly always in regard to God, helping his people. Man was like act one of a two-act play. He was isolated and made no sense without the second act, the woman. Together they make a completed whole.'

There was a pause while this point sank in.

'So you could argue that man is the helpless one, and without women he would be lost.'

'Of *course*!' The group was predominantly female.

'I've just thought of something,' said Sallie excitedly.

'Go on.'

'Well, babies come from women. So you could say that because all men originally came out of women that woman is the source and man is the, well, what comes out.'

'The issue?' suggested Gina helpfully.

'OK, the issue. But this story has it the other way round. Man is the source and woman is the issue. So it all sort of balances, doesn't it?'

'I think that's very helpful, Sallie,' said Gina. 'So if anyone wants to argue that the source is more important than the issue...'

'Or the issue than the source.'

'Exactly. You have an answer.'

Several members of the group were clearly lost at this point, but Edith was busy with her Bible.

'It's all here,' said Edith. 'Just a minute. Yes. 1 Corinthians 11:11-12, "In the Lord, however, woman is not independent of man, nor is man independent of woman. For as woman came from man, so also man is born of woman. But everything comes from God." So Paul beat Sallie to it by about 1900 years.'

Sallie was, however, delighted to find herself in such company.

At this point Timothy called for leaders to sum up, so Gina took a deep breath:

'Genesis 1:26-27 showed that, in the sight of God, men and women are exactly equal in status, responsibility and love. They are equally valuable to him and to each other.

'But Genesis 2 shows that there is a wonderful built-in richness in this relationship, so that although neither is superior to the other they are vastly different. This is not only a matter of child-bearing or even of physical differences. Woman is both necessary company and sustainer for man – she keeps him going. Man is not only first in the field, as it were, but also in need of woman.

'The relationship is like a kaleidoscope, with constantly changing patterns, but at no point are men and women identical, except in their *value* to God and to each other.'

33

Even Gina blushed when her group gave her a spontaneous round of applause.

Do you agree with Timothy's four principles?
Why?/Why not?
Do you think that they work well in practice?
Try them on some short Bible passages.

4

Behind the Vicarage curtains

Timothy put down his knife and fork and pushed away his plate.

'Aren't you hungry, darling?' asked Diana.

'Not really. There's nothing wrong with the food. It's me I suppose, or rather us. What can we do?'

'I keep telling you there's nothing wrong basically,' said Diana. 'It's just a touch of post-natal depression. That's what Stewart said.' (Stewart was the doctor.)

'It's ironical, I suppose,' said Timothy, half to himself. 'Here you have a really happy relationship that's lasted twelve years. By the grace of God we've been able to demonstrate what a good marriage looks like, not just for show, but because it really was, *is*,' he

35

added hastily. 'All that was missing was a child. And now, like Abraham and Sarah, we have been blessed with Rebecca.'

'Well, I know I'm 37, but Sarah was about 90 wasn't she? And I thought it was Isaac. Rebekah was Isaac's wife.'

Timothy sighed.

'There's no need for us to argue about the details,' he said. 'You know what I mean. Nothing could have been better. The whole church was delighted. Shelley Barber is over the moon. But as soon as Rebecca arrived everything seems to have gone wrong with us.'

'Well, it wasn't easy,' said Diana. 'For me, I mean. I often think men ought to give birth to a baby each just so that they get an idea of what it's like.'

'Yes, I know it was tough,' said her husband. 'And your age...'

'Don't keep on about my *age*, please,' said Diana testily. 'People have first babies in their forties. I'm not old.'

Diana certainly did not look old. Her brown hair had not lost its lustre over the past year and her figure had returned almost to its former slenderness. Indeed it was Timothy who was looking older than his thirty-nine years.

'Oh dear, I keep saying the wrong thing,' said Timothy helplessly. 'But before Rebecca we always seem to have been able to discuss our differences and work them out together. Now we seem to be on opposite sides all the time.'

'So I suppose that's Rebecca's fault, is it?' Diana sat up straight in defence of her daughter. 'That poor little mite is being blamed for everything.'

'No. I didn't *mean* that,' said Timothy. 'Why does everything have to be misunderstood? I meant that it's happened in the last six months, not because it's Rebecca's fault. We don't seem to be able to discuss things rationally any more.'

'Having a baby is not a rational activity,' said Diana, 'and we knew that things would never be the same in the family. They never are with three. I have to spend a lot of time with Rebecca and you feel left out, I suppose. But that's bound to happen. And if you were really as rational and reasonable as you claim to be, you'd understand that and stop arguing all the time.'

For the third time that day Diana broke down into a deluge of tears. Timothy, concerned as ever, leapt to his feet and put his arm round her shoulders.

'Don't maul me!' was all that she would say between sobs and Timothy retired, hurt and confused, to his study.

The perfect wife

What could be done? No matter how hard he tried Timothy seemed to be making matters worse. He'd tried prayer of course, affection, argument, reason, emotion, everything he could think of. What made it so hard to understand, and to bear, was the suddenness and the depth of the change. Diana had been consistently vivacious, caring, out-going and supportive. Few people could have had a more selfless wife. They had discussed everything together, not just household matters but theology and church politics. They'd enjoyed those discussions and they had often been led to greater understanding and changes, too, in the

37

church. They had prayed and read the Bible together.

In fact Diana had been as much the leader of the church as he had, thought Timothy. They'd done it together. She had worked, unpaid, and he had received the credit and the salary. But now Diana's help had been withdrawn because she was totally involved with Rebecca and her support in positive discussions was also gone, because they seemed always to be arguing. And they had given up praying together as well. And he was supposed to be the *vicar*!

He put his head in his hands and allowed waves of self-pity to wash over him.

This was ridiculous, thought Timothy. Had he not counselled many people who had to live with someone suffering from depression? Had he not told them that this is a disability, like a sort of mental or emotional accident? That it would certainly improve with time and prayer? And, above all, that one should not get emotionally drawn in oneself? It was easy, he reflected, to be wise where other people were concerned. That sort of wisdom seemed to collapse when it was one's own wife. Her emotional problems hooked into his own.

Perhaps that was it. For the fortieth time he wondered whether it was really all his own fault. Diana seemed to think so. Perhaps this change in family style had hit him, without his noticing it, and Diana had caught it from him. Where did it all end?

But it wasn't just the apparent character-change and their mixed-up relating. Diana seemed to have shot off on a new, feminist line. Perhaps 'feminist' was the wrong word, though. 'Matriarchal' might be better. She was fiercely jealous for the baby and very unwilling for

Timothy to help with bathing, changing and feeding. This was quite the opposite of their declared intention, because they believed, and told others, that fathers ought to be closely involved with children from the start.

This defensiveness spread to the house, too. She became more than ever meticulous about housekeeping, despite Timothy's anxious entreaties that she should rest. She regarded the Vicarage as her nest, he supposed, and was driving off predators, of which he was one.

It went further still. Diana had become infatuated (Timothy's word) with Proverbs 31, the account of the admirable wife, who not only organized the home establishment with superb efficiency but also got out and engaged in land transactions and was, in short, the pivot of the family's fortunes and finances.

Diana seemed to have taken this idyllic image to be a mandate for interfering (Timothy's word again) in church matters and trying to impose her own ideas on the direction the fellowship should take. Timothy resented this deeply and became defensive in his turn. To outward appearance not much had changed, but whereas Diana and Timothy had used to work things out together, it now appeared to Timothy that she was taking unwarrantable initiatives. For him the helper had become the stirrer – the ally had become the enemy.

'Enemy.' What a terrible word to use about one's own wife! Yet it had floated unbidden into his mind. He decided to ask God's forgiveness, but thought it best not to tell Diana, just now anyway.

It all began at the fall

At that moment Diana appeared at the study door with a tray.

'I'm sorry, Tim,' she said. 'Can I come and hear how you feel as well as telling you what I feel? And...and I don't mind being mauled a little.'

As he embraced Diana, Timothy reflected that these oases of peace and contentment always seemed to come just when their relationship was at breaking-point. How good of God to allow it. If only the peace could last, spread out from this moment through the rest of their lives. He was realistic enough to know that it would be short-lived. Anyway, make the most of it while you have it.

They sat down and said again how sorry they were to be hurting each other and confessed their self-pity. Timothy took the opportunity to suggest a prayer. They linked hands and expressed their feelings of wretchedness. The oasis of peace seemed to be growing.

'Why is it that we get on opposite sides so easily?' asked Diana.

'Do you think we can talk about it without getting on opposite sides?' Timothy was not optimistic.

'Well, let's try. We're on the same side now. So if one of us changes over the other must shout "Basingstoke" or something.'

'OK,' said Timothy, 'Basingstoke it is. To begin with, I don't think that it's ultimately our invention, this conflict business. It began in the Garden of Eden.'

'That doesn't mean that we're not responsible for keeping it going, though.'

'No, of course not, but it is deeply ingrained in

human nature. It's in those studies in Genesis the house groups are doing. The conclusion of that first meeting, that most people agreed, I think, was that man and woman were created absolutely equal in God's sight, because they were both in the image of God, both capable of love and both responsible beings.

'But although they were equal in value they had different functions and they related to one another differently, like a kaleidoscope, someone said. I think that sums it up, doesn't it?'

'I don't know, darling, I wasn't there. But that was what you said before.'

'Right. Well, here are these equally "godlike" people, equally loving and responsible, and they *both* disobey God.'

'Paul says it was Eve's fault really, because she fell first.'

'Well, it was Adam's fault as well. And in defence of Eve I would say that she had the whole machinery of hell to cope with. Adam was tempted only by his wife. He should have known better. Anyway they both did it. Mankind is uniformly disobedient to God. One result of that disobedience was that it showed the relationship of husband and wife and made the equal unequal.'

'Where do you get that from? Paul seemed to think that God made them unequal.'

'Let's leave Paul aside for a minute. Where I get it from is Genesis 3:16. Among all the other results of the disobedience God tells Eve, "Your desire will be for your husband, and he will rule over you." That wasn't the original idea. The equality has been upset. The fall affected every aspect of life and the way it hit the relationship was to twist it.

41

'So man is given a role which he alternately enjoys (by flexing his muscles and dominating his wife) and dislikes, because he often dodges the responsibility involved. And woman finds herself in a subservient role which she was not designed for and which she has always resented. But at the same time part of her *wants* to be dominated. If this reading is correct, that the original plan has been torn up and man and woman forced into roles that they weren't designed for, then no wonder there's a battle of the sexes. But instead of wanting equality the battle of the sexes is usually for supremacy.'

Diana was thoughtful.

'You're going to have a lot of explaining to do when we deal with what Paul says in his epistles,' said Diana slowly.

'Perhaps so,' said Timothy, 'but what I am saying is that we are in a badly warped world. Men and women are *expected* to be on opposite sides. Children are encouraged to be divisive – boys mustn't cry but may despise girls – and so it goes on. The ultimate question is, does the cross and resurrection cancel the result of the fall? Does Jesus' triumph over sin mean that we can revert to the proper relationship originally designed for the Garden of Eden? Does John 3:16 cancel Genesis 3:16?'

'You've got a sermon outline there, Vicar,' said Diana. 'And I'm not going to argue this time.'

Do you think that husbands ought to rule the household?

If husbands and wives are in competition with each other, whose fault is it? Can anything be done about it?

42

5

Life with the Rogers

Nigel whistled cheerfully as he broke another egg into a cup and tossed it nonchalantly into the sizzling mass in the pan on the cooker. Sallie would soon be home from the City and he was cooking something rather special. They needed to eat promptly, because the house group was to meet at their home that evening.

What would his mother say if she saw him now? Or his stepmother? Or his father – Lieutenant Colonel Fitzpaine Rogers? Could this really be his son, wearing a tattered pullover and jeans and a *pinafore*? And working in a tiny kitchen in a bungalow in the suburbs of London. Out of work and with a wife to support and she supporting him. Well, they supported one another, but fond parents wouldn't see it that way. But why should Nigel feel guilty? They were happy and everything was working out well.

Was it just the church that gave him these feelings of guilt about doing housework, or was it the knowledge that all his ex-colleagues in the City were probably rolling about with mirth? He'd had plenty of time to reflect on the problem but had come to no conclusion. Rationally it was obviously best for him to do the cooking and cleaning. He was at home all day, he enjoyed doing it and he couldn't help thinking that he was rather a good cook. But public opinion was still heavily prejudiced, whatever the forward-looking sociologists said, and the Bible seemed to be against him as well – at least the way the St Barnabas people saw it.

Deeply involved as he was with his thoughts and his culinary creation, he did not hear the front door and suddenly Sallie burst in upon him.

'Darling!'

'Darling!'

As he looked happily over her shoulder as they hugged one another and wondered where his spatula had fallen, he hoped that long years of marriage would never dim their delight in meeting again after ten hours apart.

'How was today, then?'

Nigel disengaged himself and stooped to pick up his spatula.

'Just another day really,' said Sallie, 'the usual problems. I've finished the Maclaren business. He agreed in the end. Sonia was a bit poisonous again.'

44

'Same as last time?'

'Yes. How noble I am to work so hard to support my husband. How hard it must be for him and all that. She doesn't mean to be nasty. It's the way she says it.'

'The problem is,' said Nigel, stirring vigorously, 'that no matter how sure we are that we're doing right it's very hard when people take it for granted that we're not.'

'Well, it is rather,' said Sallie. 'I tell them that it's not a permanent arrangement anyway and when it's clear what direction your career will be going then you'll be looking for openings. But they think that's an excuse and that you're just being lazy.'

'But what business is it of theirs if it was a permanent arrangement anyway? Who decides what we do? Popular opinion or us?'

'Or the Bible?'

'Or the Bible? And how do the three fit together?'

There was a pause while the cook served the supper.

Whose business is it?

'As far as I can see,' said Nigel, as soon as Sallie had finished congratulating him on the quality of the supper, 'there's a general fashion today to please yourself, to do whatever you want to. If you listen to the radio during the day as I do there seem to be lots of discussion programmes and the "experts" they invite are usually trendy thinkers and sociologists. They positively sneer at any kind of guiding principles. They're very keen on the right of individuals to decide their own future. The rights of the woman over her own body in the abortion debate is a prime example. But it goes much wider. Things that interfere with what you think is best for you, duties, responsibilities, tradition, most of all religious principles, are just dismissed as beneath contempt. So if we follow the popular trend...'

'We say fiddlesticks to what other people think or to any truth we might have picked up from the past and do our own thing,' said Sallie, who was becoming anxious that Nigel would get so carried away with the subject that he would neglect his supper. But Nigel was already in full flow and had laid down his knife and fork.

'Exactly,' he said. 'It's all clear and straightforward in theory. There's this great pressure to conform to the trendy view and just do what fulfils your own needs.

'*But*, there seems to be another equal pressure coming from the other direction, which demands adherence to traditional values. Mothers should stay at home and look after their children. Abortion is shocking. Homosexuality is disgusting. Husbands *ought* to be out at work. You know it all. People who take those views occasionally write to the press, but they're not invited to radio debates. The pressure comes through remarks made by Sonia and people like her. Our parents, too. There's an atmosphere of, what shall I say, disapproval, even when people don't say anything.

'So we're all caught in the crossfire between these two forces. They're quite opposite to each other and we're torn in two by them. No wonder people suffer from depression.'

'And indigestion,' said Sallie quickly, as Nigel drew breath. 'Look, I've finished already and your supper's getting cold and the people will be here in less than half an hour. You eat and let me tell you what I think.'

'Are you going to wait till I'm eating so that you can

tell me I'm wrong?'

'Oh, no, I think you're right so far. You've described the situation very well. The appalling thing is that people accept either the trendy view or the traditional one without question. If you ask either side what basic grounds they have for believing what they do, they would probably splutter and tell you that it's obvious and make you feel silly for having dared to ask the question. But neither of them have any real foundation.

'The self-fulfilment idea seems to come from American psychologists, as far as I can see, and the traditional view is a kind of pale reflection of Christian values mixed up with middle-class custom. So there are two opposite views, both based on half-digested and vague opinions but both exalted to the rank of dogma by the way people talk in hushed tones as if it was obviously true.'

It was Nigel's turn to get worried that his wife was getting carried away.

'What's your solution, then?' he asked, collecting the plates.

'To ask the basic question of course, "Whose business is it how we live our lives, our own or other people's?" And the answer is that it's God's business. At least we've cooked up a few questions for this evening's meeting.'

'A thoroughly representative group'

It was Gina Renshaw's group that met in the Rogers' house. There were seven members. Gina herself, Edith Kent, Nigel, Sallie, Mrs Beesley from 'The Haven', the sheltered accommodation for old people, and a friend of hers called Elsie Boggett, who usually said nothing but occasionally made a remark which was either wildly off the point or very profound. The seventh member of the group on this occasion was Carol Jenkins, on vacation from university. The age range was 19 to 77. It was what some would call a 'thoroughly representative group'. Others, including Gina, thought of it as too mixed-up to be of any use, and with only one man.

It took some time for the group to settle. Mrs Beesley had to be not too near the fire but not too far from it, even though it was a warm evening. Elsie's hearing-aid needed a great deal of attention and Edith Kent then started a long recital of a visit she and her husband had made last summer to York and, as she was addressing the whole meeting, it was difficult to interrupt. At length she paused for breath and Sallie quickly suggested that Gina should begin.

She waved a sheet of paper, written all over in Timothy's tidy handwriting. 'Timothy's been busy working out an outline on this,' she said, 'so I'm passing on some of what he suggests.' She reminded them of the general theme, 'Male and female, who's in charge?' and that they had established that, in the beginning, as recorded in Genesis, Adam and Eve had been equally created 'in God's image' and had been perfectly complementary to one another.

'That is how it should be,' she went on; 'every man and every woman ought to have their own place in society where they can use the gifts God has given them. They were given a joint stewardship in the Garden of Eden, equally in charge. But some jobs are more suitable for men to do...'

'I wouldn't mind being a coal-miner or a professional boxer,' interrupted Carol.

'Thank you Carol,' said Gina with exaggerated polite-
ness, 'I think you have made my point for me. Some
jobs are equally open to either sex. What is needed is
mutual respect so that we can support each other.'
Nigel and Sallie exchanged glances.

'But it isn't like that,' said Mrs Beesley, 'there's no
respect for anybody today. I was telling her the other
day, wasn't I Mrs Boggett?, about that young man on
the 34 bus into town, or was it the 34A, I can't
remember...'

'Exactly,' said Gina, 'it's all gone wrong. That is why
our subject today is the fall. Genesis chapter 3.'
Somehow the chapter was shared between them and
remarks about different Bible versions dealt with. The
old story of the serpent, the temptation, Eve's falling for
the fruit and Adam's following her was read again and
considered.

'What we're concerned about,' said Gina, 'is the effect
the fall had on the relationship between the man and
the woman. Look at chapter 3 verse 16. It looks as if
childbearing was supposed to be easy, but now it would
become difficult. Then it says, "your desire will be for
your husband." My commentary says that this may
mean that her sexual desire had now become a grasping
urge, perhaps to manipulate her husband for her own
satisfaction*. The husband will now dominate his wife,
instead of being her "opposite number" and equal. So
we have the picture of the whole relationship spoilt.
Love becomes lust, responsibility becomes domination.

*Gina was referring to the Bible Speaks Today volume, *The Message
of Genesis 1-11*, by David Atkinson, p.94, published by IVP. It is not
technically a commentary but an exposition – however, we must
forgive her. D.W.

God is saying that this is a curse. It's not as it should be. It's not what he planned it to be. Adam and Eve have brought this on themselves. A balanced and wholesome relationship has become lop-sided and selfish...'

'This is just what we were talking about before you came,' said Sallie. 'We were looking at all this lop-sidedness – some people saying that the woman's place is in the home, and some saying that women should be fulfilled by being free, and nobody really having real authority for their views. So are you saying that there is no authority for gender roles because the fall has muddled everything up for ever?'

Gender roles

At this point there was a break in the discussion, because Elsie's hearing-aid was not equal to coping with 'gender roles' and it had to be explained to her that men and women have traditionally had different parts to play both in society and in marriage.

'Of course they have,' she said, when all had become clear, 'and quite right too. But it doesn't mean that one of them should lord it over the other.' This, being one of Elsie's more rational statements, was applauded.

It was decided, after a great deal of discussion, that men and women did indeed have different functions and roles, but that those roles could not be decided for all time. In different times and in different cultures what was 'right' for women, or 'right' for men, might change. It was agreed, however, that men and women must not expect to have exactly the same roles as each other. If, through circumstances or choice, a man found himself housekeeper and cook (Nigel beamed broadly), it was not necessary for his wife to be doing the same thing, except where it was helpful to share the load.

It was also suggested that whether the husband kept house or was the 'breadwinner' did not affect the general question as to who should lead. If it was right for the man to be the boss, then he could be boss from the kitchen just as well as from his office desk. This provoked a storm of protest, mainly from Carol, who saw 'being chained to the hot stove' as a degrading and subservient task, and from Edith, who approved of the woman keeping her place in the kitchen but thought that the person who worked for a wage, the husband, ought to be in charge of how it was used. Carol thought that was thoroughly unjust, as the person who worked for most of her waking hours, *without a wage*, was much more noble and should have the authority to compensate her for having no income.

At this point Gina decided that they were getting off the point and Nigel suggested coffee.

'We must sum up first.' Gina was anxious that some kind of progress should be seen to be made. 'We've agreed that what women or men do just because they are women or men is still open to discussion. The Bible doesn't say that men mustn't wash up or women mustn't drive lorries. Of course not.

'What we have established this evening, though, is that the original ease of relationship between Adam and Eve was totally spoilt by the fall and we have all inherited a twisted view of each other. The "battle of the sexes" began in the Garden of Eden. There's a kind of love-hate relationship between women and men, longing for each other and needing each other, yet fighting for supremacy and trying to cut each other down to size. Men have generally won the battles because men are stronger and have established themselves in society as leaders. Women have fought back, especially recently, but neither has won the war.

'We haven't established yet who is supposed to be the leader, but we have seen how the struggle started, and how futile it all is.'

'But surely,' Sallie broke in, 'that's a very pessimistic idea. Haven't Christians at least something better to hope for?'

'Yes, I think we have,' said Gina. 'Thank you for putting us back on track. That's the subject of the next meeting: "Does John 3:16 reverse Genesis 3:16?" Homework is to look up the verses and come with some ideas.'

Is it true that what men or women do, in house, garden or workplace, has no bearing on who should lead in society or family?

If the domination of man over woman as we have seen it in history is in fact a curse (Genesis 3:16), how can we discover what is the right relationship?

6

Disaster!

Diana found herself humming a tune as she washed the coffee cups. It was good to feel better, even for a short time. It was another golden autumn morning and life seemed to be returning to normal again.

Timothy was in London, attending a day conference, and Diana had just waved goodbye to Jane Goodrich, who had been pouring out some of her problems. It was odd, thought Diana, that hearing someone else's problems, loss of mother, uncertainty as to what to do next, arthritis, partial loss of faith even, all this could leave one feeling easier about one's own difficulties. Perhaps she hadn't been really concerned enough about Jane. Surely she ought to be feeling deeply moved by Jane's story. But, no, she had been of use by letting Jane open her mind, and feelings, and that was good.

Everything was good suddenly. Timothy was much happier since their evening talk and Rebecca was a constant delight. Dear little Becky. She must be still asleep outside on the patio. It would soon be time for her to come in. Diana tiptoed round the corner of the house. Would that little face be peering up, those two bright eyes eager to see her again?

The pram was not there.

There was no sign of it. Diana glanced quickly round the garden, but of course the pram could not have moved itself. Becky had been stolen! In a flash Diana saw herself making tearful appeals on television, urging the young childless woman to return her baby. Or even worse, the scheming criminal who might hold Becky to ransom. Would the Church Commissioners have a million pounds to spare? Even as these thoughts raced through her mind Diana's fingers were pressing nine three times on the telephone. 'Police! Police! I've lost my baby!'

Had she really put Becky outside?

As she replaced the receiver Diana reproached herself for doing things in the wrong order. She should have run to the front gate first. The thief might still be in sight. Accordingly she ran through the kitchen, out of the back door and up the short gravel path to the front gate. As usual the High Road was full of traffic, the pavements thronged with people. Which way could the thief have gone? To the left it was a hundred yards to the crossroads and any one of three directions. To the right it was a hundred yards and across the pedestrian crossing to the station. And trains ran into London every few minutes. Becky could be anywhere already. Had anyone seen a baby in a pram? Yes, of course, plenty of them. The whole of Canwell Park was full of them.

She was tempted to rush across to the station and had visions of snatching Becky back from her captor just as the train's doors were closing. Then she remembered that the Vicarage door was open and that she was expecting the police to come. And what about Timothy? He should be told. She ran back to the house and left a message at the conference centre to ask her husband to call back as soon as possible.

Only then did she allow herself to sit down and try to collect her thoughts. Had she really put Becky outside? Yes, of course she had. In the back garden, well out of sight of the road and opposite the window so that she could see the pram all the time she had been talking to Jane. Yes, they had both looked out of the window and noticed that Becky was asleep. She appeared to be holding her teddy. So no-one could have taken the pram away while Jane and Diana had been talking. Neither could they have done so while Diana was washing the cups, because the sink was next to the open back door and there was no other entrance to the back garden.

What had happened when she said goodbye to Jane? She had walked to the gate with her and then... and *then* she had gone back into the house and to the bathroom, before washing the cups. So in those few seconds, while her back had been turned, the thief had come in. How could anyone have known that Becky was there? The park was on the other side of the garden, but there was a seven-foot-high brick wall between them. Who would climb high walls looking for possible babies to steal? No, only two people in the world knew where Becky was, herself and Jane. And she had seen Jane to the gate.

At that moment the doorway was darkened by the appearance of a man and a woman in police uniform and Diana collapsed in a confusion of tears.

Her eye strayed to the open window

Jane had been very grateful to Diana for listening to her problems. She hated bothering people with her difficulties ('they have enough of their own, without having mine as well'), but Diana *was* the Vicar's wife and she did seem genuinely sympathetic. She even told her about Bob's surprising attempt to be helpful. Diana nodded very knowingly.

But despite the coffee and the understanding and the warm autumn sunshine, life still seemed totally unreal to Jane. She seemed to be looking in at herself from outside. She watched herself stirring her coffee. She heard Diana's voice but felt that someone else was being addressed. Even when she was describing her own experiences she seemed to be telling a story about someone else. The only reality seemed to be the baby. Becky was a slice of real life, somehow, not spoilt by the tragedies of living. It had been a high moment when they had looked together to see whether Becky was asleep. Jane listened to Diana and spoke to her almost mechanically, while her eye every now and then strayed to the open window.

Jane had never seriously admitted to herself that she had longed for a child. She had told her mother that she would like to be married, when was it, forty years ago now. And mother had not opposed the idea. Not exactly. 'Very well, dear, you have your own life to lead. I can't always expect you to be running round after me. I have been expecting this sort of thing ever since your father died. No, it has to be. We can't put the clock back. We must all be prepared to suffer. I won't stand in your way, you know that. You must do what is best for *you*. That's what matters. I shall be all right, I suppose. You mustn't mind me.'

Harold, the young man who was indirectly the cause of this torrent of selfless devotion, had had to be told that if he married Jane then he married her mother as well and that was too much even for the noble Harold to contemplate. He retired gracefully and found a comfortable widow in Wimbledon.

Since then Jane had been continually on duty, attending to all her mother's needs, great and small. And deep down she had longed for a husband, a family, to care for someone she loved instead of feeling this duty to care for someone she ought to honour because she was her mother.

When Jane reached the High Road and had thanked Diana for the coffee and the talk, she realized that she had not said goodbye to Becky. What an omission! The dear little scrap might be awake by now. Jane longed for just one more peep at those eyes. So she retraced her steps and hesitated at the back door. She gave a faint knock and said softly, 'Diana dear, I'm just going to say goodbye to Becky.' Diana, of course, did not hear.

Becky was, in fact, just awakening and produced one of those yawns which babies and all small animals seem to have in common, a kind of helpless dependence on whoever is near, endearing in the extreme. Jane could never explain what happened next. All she knew was that for the time being she and Becky belonged together. Perhaps God had sent the baby into her life to help her over her problems. Dreamily she released the brake on the pram and wheeled it down the path, turned left and left again into Highwood Avenue and made for home in Fairview Avenue, as proud as any grandmother.

What is reality?

Later on Jane was still bewildered by these events. She remembered being convinced that Becky and she were the only reality and everything and everyone else were a dream. She walked happily homewards, gazing often into the pram and convincing herself that Becky was smiling at her (when in fact she was somewhat dazzled by the sun).

All went well until Margaret Barber suddenly appeared before her, hurrying to do some morning shopping. Jane felt the need to run away, but couldn't remember why, so decided to brazen it out.

'Hello Jane,' said Margaret, 'has Diana given you the job of nursemaid then?'

'Well, er, yes, I suppose she has,' said Jane uncertainly, looking round and apparently recognizing where she was, almost as if awaking from sleep. The realization of what she was doing was dawning on Jane and she felt first embarrassed, then ashamed, and then very frightened.

'I think we've gone far enough now, haven't we?' said Jane to the uncomprehending Rebecca. 'Let's go home to Mummy now.'

Margaret offered to accompany them the quarter of a mile back to the Vicarage. She asked Jane a few questions about her unexpected role as baby-walker, but Jane was non-committal. Her mind was on Diana. She was longing, hoping, desperately praying that Diana would have been busy with something else and not have noticed that Becky was missing. Perhaps even now she could get Margaret to distract Diana's attention and slip the pram back to its original position. How long had she been away? Ten, fifteen minutes? Diana might easily have had a telephone call or a visitor...

But as they rounded the corner by the 'Auld Alliance' and came in view of the Vicarage her heart sank to zero. Just drawing up at the gate was a police patrol car and out of it climbed a policewoman followed by a policeman. They both walked up the Vicarage path in a very businesslike way.

Who was to blame for Becky's disappearance?
What would you say to Jane if you could meet her now at the Vicarage gate?
What would you say to Diana?

59

7

Dominoes on Thursdays

'**I** don't know whether that meeting at our house got us anywhere, really.'

Sallie and Nigel were walking hand in hand, on their way to an evening with the Barbers. Was it really only last year when they had first visited the Barbers? On that occasion they had roared round in Sallie's TR7, she dressed to kill and he armed with a bottle to impress. They had gone from their expensive town house in Canwell Gardens. Now they were coming from the opposite direction, from 'the estate', an area of small bungalows and high-rise flats. And they were walking. But they were going to visit not Gordon and Margaret, those stuffy, church-going people, but Gordon and

Margaret their warm friends. Anyway, if you walked to save petrol you also had time to talk.

'Oh, I don't know,' said Nigel, using the same words as Sallie and meaning the opposite. 'I think it was quite helpful. We got it clear that the headship of the male was the result of the fall. In other words, God meant everyone to be equal and we've gone and spoilt it.'

'No, I don't think that was what we said,' said Sallie. 'In any case that would make all Paul's stuff about obedience and submission completely cock-eyed. We haven't come to that yet. No. I think it's more subtle than what you said just now. It looks as if there was a *right* kind of leadership for the male which God intended, but the fall made it into the *wrong* kind. What we're trying to do is to find out what the right kind of leadership is, for all time, and how we can apply it to our own situation here.'

'Fair enough,' said Nigel amicably, 'and meanwhile we carry on as we are, sharing the jobs and sharing the leadership until we know what's right.'

'OK, and asking other people what they do about it. Perhaps we shall get a chance to quiz Gordon and Margaret this evening. What I can't understand is Timothy and Diana. Timothy is the Vicar and he's producing all the material for this Bible study course, so I suppose he knows it all – he's got all the answers. So why doesn't it work in practice for them? Is it worth knowing all the theory if you can't make it work in real life? Ignorance might be bliss after all.'

'I think that's a bit hard, Sallie,' said Nigel, as they dodged a taxi which had suddenly made a 180-degree turn in the middle of Highwood Avenue and sped off in the opposite direction. 'She's had an awful lot of trouble with this depression business. And now Jane and the baby. Diana was just getting a bit better, so Tim told me, but this bother with Jane has plunged her right back to square one.'

'Yes, I think that's awful,' admitted Sallie. 'And poor Jane. What got into her? She's under sedation now, so Gina said. They're not letting the police go any further with it of course, but who's going to look after Jane? She has no relatives.'

'Gina, I suppose,' said Nigel. 'Whenever anything needs doing, call on the Barbers or Gina.'

'And there they are!' said Sallie as they turned into the Barbers' front garden. Walking down the other side of the avenue, rather clumsily because he had his arm locked firmly round her waist, were Gina and Bob Renshaw.

The 'Auld Alliance' again

While Nigel and Sallie were spending the evening with the Barbers, Bob and Gina were going to the 'Auld Alliance', the hostelry on the corner by the War Memorial. It was a very well-run establishment with a restaurant at the back, bar meals available to all, only one fruit machine and only soft background music. There was always a quiet welcome and some people rather unkindly said that you were made to feel more at home there than in the church next door.

But Gina was deeply unhappy to be accompanying Bob on that particular evening. Bachelor Bob had had a small group of friends who met regularly every Thursday evening in 'the Snuggery' off the chief room in the Alliance and, over a few half-pints of beer, they had played dominoes. Over the years, Bob's quiet faith had impressed this little group and one of them, Stanley, had become a regular church-goer and one other had come occasionally. So Bob was able to justify his weekly visit, not only on the grounds of habit and tradition but also because it was a proper extension of the church's witness. Didn't the Salvation Army do likewise? And after their marriage, Bob had asked Gina to accompany him. It seemed wrong to him that she should be left at home while he reverted to his bachelor habits, and it never occurred to him to withdraw from the Thursday group, 'the lads' as the silvery-haired and balding members of the party called themselves.

Gina had no quarrel with public houses in general and she was more than happy for Bob to continue his Thursday evening get-together. In fact she had looked forward to the opportunity to be quiet at home. Bob was being somewhat possessive, wanting her with him all the time and, after years of living alone, the strain was beginning to tell on her. So Gina's heart sank when Bob proposed that she should accompany him on Thursdays. The other 'lads' were very polite, but it was clear that they resented Gina's presence and jumped to the conclusion that she was unwilling to let Bob out of her sight. Having failed to persuade him to stay at home, they assumed, she was keeping an eye on him. All this was unspoken but fairly obvious. The fact that nothing could be further from the truth made it all the harder to bear.

Gina was not expected to join in the game and had to spend the evening rather miserably in a corner of the Snuggery with a book and a glass of mineral water. When Bob asked her whether she was happy she smiled bravely and said yes. He believed her and went on contentedly with his game.

Return to the bar

No, Gina was not happy. She had two further reasons for unhappiness to add to the foregoing.

The 'Auld Alliance' had left a very unpleasant taste in Gina's memory. Two years previously she had attended a party there, as chronicled elsewhere (*The Simon Peter file*), and had allowed herself to drink too much. The combination of alcohol and the tablets she had been taking for depression had had a disastrous effect and she had been discovered in the early hours of the morning, clinging to a pillar box and singing Scripture choruses at the top of her voice.

The people of Canwell Park had laughed and generously forgotten the incident. The people of St Barnabas' church had wept and most of them had forgiven her. Indeed Gina herself had felt that she was stronger for the experience, after she had forgiven herself and understood the warmth of the fellowship in receiving her back (had she ever been away?), and seen it as a symbol of God's acceptance.

But she had never been back to the 'Auld Alliance'. It was easy to tell someone who fell off a bicycle to get on it again at once and regain their confidence, but it was not so easy for Gina Renshaw to return to the bar. The bar? Was it a judgment of some kind?

So why had she not refused to go? She wanted to be at home. Surely Bob would have been happier with his friends without her? This was the second additional reason for Gina's unhappiness. For Bob had made an issue of it and had appealed to the wedding vows in which Gina had undertaken to obey him. He had appealed also to the teaching of the apostle Paul in his letter to the Ephesians, 'Wives, submit to your husbands as to the Lord' (Ephesians 5:22).

Gina had responded spiritedly that the next paragraph ordered husbands to love their wives, 'just as Christ loved the church and gave himself up for her.' Wasn't this a balance to the order to the wives to submit?

Yes it was, but this was not a bargain or legalistic agreement. It didn't say, 'wives, submit to your husbands, *provided that they are as loving as Christ was to the church.*' The wife's task was to submit. The husband's responsibility was to love. It was a high calling and Bob recognized that he was not as good at it as he might be, but there it was and that was what the Scripture said.

'Submit to one another'?

What kind of love was it, Gina wanted to know, that dictated how it should be dispensed without reference to whether the wife wanted to be loved in that way? Jesus loves the church for the church's benefit. He knows what is good for it. Surely Bob was not claiming to be omniscient and able to judge what kind of love was best for his wife without consulting her? Who did he think he was, dispensing 'love' in this high-handed way? Was it loving to be so condescending?

Bob had incautiously reminded her that the kind of love demanded from a husband was of a very high order. The shepherd may be called even to sacrifice himself for his sheep.

Gina retorted that she was not a sheep but a human being, and what kind of sacrifice was it for Bob to order her about? Then she had produced what she saw as her trump card. Did it not say in Ephesians 5 verse 21, 'submit *to one another* out of reverence for Christ'?

But Bob had done his homework and was ready for that argument. Mostly the commentaries were agreed that 'submit to one another' was the conclusion of the previous paragraph about giving thanks to God for everything. Then Paul began a new paragraph and a new subject with the words, 'Wives, submit to your husbands.' So you couldn't argue from verse 21 that husbands should also submit to wives.

At this point it was clear that they would get nowhere further. Gina reflected sadly that you could make the Bible say what you wanted it to say, and Bob responded that it was crystal clear what it said in this case.

A willow tree

Perhaps these more liberal thinkers were right after all, thought Gina, as she stared moodily into her empty mineral water glass. Perhaps we were wrong to take the teaching of Paul so seriously. After all he was living in a society which treated women as little better than slaves. Things have changed enormously since then. We *have* to interpret the New Testament in the light of the conditions of society at the time. It's only reasonable and loving.

Loving? How loving was Bob being to drag her down here? Then, how loving was she being in not making allowances for his good intentions, his strong faith, his devotion to the truth of the Bible and his clear intention to do right as he saw it? Why was it all so *difficult*? Jesus said, 'the truth shall make you free', yet the harder they tried to live by the truth the less free they seemed to be.

Gina muttered a few words of apology and walked out of the back door into the garden. She found a seat in a sheltered corner, under a willow tree, where she could weep undisturbed.

Do Paul's (and Peter's) calls for wives to submit to husbands really carry weight today?
Was Gina being rebellious and unreasonable?
Was Bob being stubborn and unjust?
What is the way out of their dilemma?
How would you advise them?

8

Tilting the Bible

'**I**f *we* can't agree about anything, how can we expect anyone else to?'

Timothy put down his pen in despair. He and Diana had booked the morning together to plan the forthcoming church family enrichment weekend. The idea was to follow up the house group meetings with a weekend away at a small conference centre in the country. A speaker had been booked to help them to clarify their ideas, and the next step was to plan the programme.

The theme was to be 'finding our roles', a chance for everyone to work out how they fitted in to the rest of their family, father, mother, children; who was to lead and who was to follow; how to dovetail the gifts that everyone had and how to make allowance for one another's failings. A tall order for one short weekend!

The 'singles' were not forgotten either, because part of the programme was to be given over to relationships within the wider family of the church. Those who lived alone, single parents, retired people living in 'The Haven', in fact everyone else, were eligible to come and find their own particular slot or niche. That was the theory that had been put forward by the church committee. It sounded exciting. On paper it looked like being the best church conference they had ever had. Timothy and Diana had been given the task of being a sub-committee to plan the details and put them before the committee. And now the difficulties were beginning to appear.

'I'll just go and see if Becky's all right.' Diana got up from the table for the fourth time and went into the next room where the baby was sleeping peacefully. She came back quickly, closed the door and stood with her back to it, ashen-faced.

'Darling,' she said urgently. 'Come and look at her. I don't think she's breathing.'

Timothy rose wearily. Ever since Jane Goodrich had 'borrowed' Becky Diana had been in a state of acute anxiety. Timothy had lost count of the number of times she had got up in the night to see whether Becky was 'all right'. The pram was never left in the garden now, although the weather was still pleasantly warm, and there was no question of Diana having time off. She would not even leave Becky with Timothy. Everything seemed to have gone back to the beginning, and worse. Believing that Becky had stopped breathing was a fairly regular occurrence. Timothy once more assured himself, if not his wife, that the baby was perfectly well and happy, and they made themselves a cup of coffee and tried again to concentrate on the forthcoming weekend.

Slaves and wives

Timothy's exasperated comment that they could not agree about anything was, of course, an exaggeration born of annoyance. The immediate question before them looked innocent enough. Should the speaker give an address first, setting the scene for them, or should they hear reports from their groups, have a debate about it and then ask the visiting 'expert' to sum up for them?

Timothy proposed the former plan. In fact the 'expert' was a 'double bill', a couple who would share the speaking and be available for private consultation. Diana opposed this idea.

'The problem is that these people will put across the traditional line at the beginning. You know, "the woman's place is in the home", "submit to your husbands" and all that. And when they've said all that we shall all feel guilty if we say anything different.'

'But you don't know that they'll take that line,' said Timothy. 'They've had lots of experience in speaking at this sort of conference. They've been asked to come and be facilitators, to help us to work out what *we* believe. I only want them to set the scene for us.'

'But that's just my point,' said Diana. 'Whatever they say at the beginning will put us either on the attack or the defensive, depending on which side we feel we're on. And from what I've read in their books I think I'm going to be on the attack.'

'What makes you say that?'

'Well, I've been thinking and reading since our last session, you know about the fall producing the domination of the male – relationships getting all twisted. And the more I've thought about it, the more I agree with you...'

'Thank goodness for small mercies,' said Timothy.

'...the more I agree with you about that one point. The fall was responsible for male supremacy and female servility. It's as clear as daylight. Man and woman were created exactly equal in every respect...'

'I never said *that*,' said Timothy guardedly.

'No, but I did. "In the image of God he created them." Exactly equal. And ever since they went wrong with the disobedience there has been a battle of the sexes, children have been rebellious against their parents, widows have been neglected by society. You name it. It all fits in.'

'But I seem to remember that you warned *me* about my idea, which you have just over-simplified, by the way, on the grounds that Paul's letters were all part of the Bible and he tells wives to submit and so on.'

'Yes, and I've been doing some reading on that, too. I opened my Bible at 1 Peter 3 to check on Peter's wording and it's almost the same as Paul's, "Wives, be submissive to your husbands" and all that. Now by a complete coincidence in this particular version the column exactly opposite says, "Slaves, submit yourselves to your masters."

'I thought, "yes, isn't that typical? Paul would have agreed on that too. Wives and slaves were just about on a level with one another in those days. The same words

71

are used to describe their relationship with their 'masters'."

'But wait a minute. How do we square that with the present-day situation? Slavery is out. Three cheers for the biblical work of Wilberforce and Shaftesbury, we say. How could any real Christian countenance one person demanding another to submit to him or her as in slavery? Of course in New Testament times slavery was the everyday norm, so Peter and Paul and the rest swallowed it and suggested ways of living Christianly despite it. It's even suggested, isn't it, that Paul's letter to Philemon is getting near to proposing that slaves should be freed.

'But what about the submission of wives to husbands? "Oh, that's different," they say. But how? How can it be a triumph of biblical living to free the slaves and keep the wives under submission at the same time? "Society has changed," we say, so "slaves, be submissive to your masters" no longer applies. Well, society has changed in its attitude to wives, so perhaps "wives, be submissive to your husbands" no longer applies either.'

Timothy opened his mouth to speak and closed it again. A sleepy cry from the next room saved him from having to argue the point any further.

'They all believe that Scripture holds all the answers'

While Gina Renshaw had been suffering silently in the 'Auld Alliance', Nigel and Sallie were greatly enjoying their evening with Gordon and Margaret Barber.

After supper, having talked of many things and

cleared away (Nigel was told to sit down and have the evening free from domestic chores), they relaxed in the Barbers' comfortable sitting-room and Nigel asked his question.

'Do you mind telling us how you two work out this "headship in marriage" business? You know us pretty well and you know that we don't have much Christian background, well, none at all, and we really do want to get this thing in the right perspective.'

'The house group meetings and the family weekend are tailor-made for you,' put in Margaret.

'Yes, they are,' said Sallie, 'but it all moves so slowly and logically and carefully. We shall be firmly set in our ways by the time the course has finished and then it'll be too late.'

'I can't imagine you two as Darby and Joan,' said Gordon, but Nigel was not to be put off by the banter.

'No, I mean this seriously,' he said. 'We've joined this church and it's a very good one, but there doesn't seem to be any clear teaching about roles in life. Not only that, but we get very different messages from different people. On the one hand there's Gina and Bob and they don't agree, really. He's trying to prove something by bossing her around...'

'Nige!' said Sallie softly.

'Well, I'm sorry, I know you're a great friend of Gina's, Margaret, but it looks like that sometimes. And it just doesn't suit them both. Then on the other hand Diana seems to be going so far down the women's lib. road that she's almost out of sight. Poor old Timothy doesn't know what's hit him. They all believe that Scripture holds all the answers and they all quote it often enough, but they come to different conclusions.

We're not happy with either extreme. So we've come to you to find out how you do it, because you seem to be the most balanced and well-orientated couple we know.'

At this Margaret blushed and Gordon shifted uncomfortably in his chair. Both were remembering the painful evening they had spent the day before in total disagreement about whether their daughter Shelley should be allowed to go to a rock party. Since they had not agreed and saw no hope of compromise, the question had been who was boss. Margaret had not promised to 'obey' Gordon at their marriage and neither was she willing to accept that in all matters Gordon's views should prevail. The matter was still not decided.

Gordon decided that honesty was of the essence, so he told Nigel and Sallie what had happened and rather apologetically concluded that he and Margaret were perhaps not the best people to come to for advice.

'But how often does this sort of thing happen?' asked Sallie.

'About once every five years.'

'So what happens the rest of the time?'

'Well, we don't think about it too much, I suppose,' said Margaret. 'Gordon decides about financial matters because that's his job anyway, but he always talks to me about it first. I deal with household things because I enjoy it. He does the garden because he likes it. We usually agree about where to go for holidays after we've talked about it. I think we take the lead where we have gifts or preferences and the other doesn't mind.'

'The only real question', said Gordon, 'is not whether Margaret or I am boss, but whether we or Shelley rule the roost.'

'So how do you work all that out from Scripture?' asked Nigel earnestly.

Gordon thought for a moment. 'I don't think we do, to be honest. We just work out problems as they come and react together. It nearly always works. I suppose we ought to be more biblical.'

'I thought we were,' said Margaret, 'but I'm not sure now.'

A question unanswered

'One big difficulty', said Gordon slowly, and Gordon was always worth listening to when he spoke slowly, 'is that fashions change regarding Bible interpretation. To some extent people do see in it what they want to see.

'Take the Genesis story, for instance. In the sixteenth or seventeenth centuries it was crystal clear to most people, including women, that the man was head of the household. It was also clear that Adam was created before Eve, that she was taken out of his side and was therefore a kind of spare part, that she fell to the serpent's temptation and that she was therefore a pretty poor helper, which is what she was there for. That fitted in well with the current ideas of the day.

'In the nineteen-nineties, however, we come at it from another angle. Equality is in the air. So we notice that God made *them* in his own image, and which came first doesn't matter. We look at the word "helper" and discover that it means "completer" or "complementary half", not a servant. We notice that Eve was taken from Adam's *side*, near his heart, rather than from his head or his foot. Love is intended. Eve fell first, but Adam fell as well, so they both fell together. Male domination comes with the fall and was not originally intended.

'You see what I mean. Depending on which way you tilt the text, it reflects different lights. And the fashion of the age is not the only criterion. The mood or predisposition of the individual makes a lot of difference. Bob and Diana are coming at it from totally opposite angles. And they are tending to find what they are looking for. What you see in the Bible can easily be a reflection of your own predigested world-view.'

'So there's no hope of our ever getting at what it's really saying,' said Sallie helplessly.

'I didn't say we can *never* discover what the Bible is saying, only that it's hard.'

'You can say that again,' said Nigel, rubbing his chin. 'So what are the rules for success?'

Sallie looked at her watch.

'Some of us have to work in the morning,' she said. 'I think we ought to be going.'

Before Nigel and Margaret could protest she tactfully added, 'Nigel and Margaret both have housework to do, so we mustn't keep them up all night.'

Nigel's question remained for the moment unanswered.

Are slavery and wifely submission in the same category?
Why/why not?
Do we normally find in the Bible what we bring to it already? Do we tilt it so that it reflects our own views?
How can we guard against this?

76

9

Home, church and government as well

'It would have to start raining now, just when I've got the whole journey to do.'

Edith Kent sighed as she parked her bulging basket-on-wheels and put up her umbrella. The 'whole journey' was no more than half a mile, but it was uphill. She noticed that hill now. Seventy-six wasn't all that old, but she'd noticed the hill recently. Highwood Avenue had seemed flat enough when Cyril was with her. He always used to come shopping with her, since he retired that is. But Cyril had recently had a stroke and was confined to the house.

Edith had finished her shopping and called at 'The Haven' to see Mrs Beesley (and to have a rest and a cup of tea), so she had even further to walk than usual. She had balanced the umbrella to her satisfaction and had set the wheeled basket in motion when a young woman crossed the road from the station and paused, looking this way and that, clearly lost.

'Can I help you, dear?' Edith was always ready to assist.

'I'm looking for the Vicarage actually,' said the young woman. 'Almost opposite the station, they said.'

'Come along,' said Edith, 'I'm just going past the Vicarage. It's only a few yards. We can go together. Are you going to see Timothy or Diana or both of them?'

Her companion started. 'You know them, then?'

'Oh yes. My husband, Cyril, he's the elder at the church. They only have one and he's had a stroke now, but yes, we're very much involved with the church.'

'Oh well, it's no secret I expect. My name's Sue and I'm going to have lunch with the Monteiths.' Sue extended her hand and turned to shake Edith's. This proved impossible, as both of her hands were occupied with basket and umbrella, but in the confusion Edith noticed that Sue was wearing a clerical collar.

'Anyway, this is the Vicarage,' she said, as she put up her umbrella again, 'Have a nice lunch. Goodbye.'

'Whatever would Cyril say?'

Edith forgot the rain and almost forgot that she was walking uphill. Whatever would Cyril say? The ordination of women was one of his favourite topics. And he was very much against it. Now what was this Sue doing, coming to the Vicarage for lunch? There had been some talk of St Barnabas' having a curate. Timothy needed help. But a woman! What*ever* would Cyril say?

Cyril, in fact, had a great deal to say, as Edith had expected. His stroke had left him with a clumsy left arm and a limp in the left leg, but his speech and his brain were unimpaired. Edith sometimes reflected that he compensated for lack of mobility by talking more than ever.

'Yes, I know it's the way the church is going, but that only makes matters worse,' Cyril was saying. 'If the whole Church of England or all the churches in the world decided to ordain women that wouldn't make it *right*. The only authority we have is the Bible.'

'But the Bible doesn't say anything about the ordination of men, either,' said Edith mildly. 'What's all the fuss about?'

'No, it's not ordination that worries me. I don't believe that ordination gives a man any special virtue that the laity don't possess. There's no magic in it. From that point of view it doesn't matter.'

'The Roman Catholics and a lot of Anglicans wouldn't agree.'

'No, but I'm not a Catholic nor a lot of Anglicans,' said Cyril firmly, not to be deflected from his train of thought. 'My problem is with the authority question. Paul is quite clear, "I suffer not a woman to teach, nor to usurp authority over the man, but to be in silence" (1 Timothy 2:12).' Cyril had a fund of quotations from the King James' Version of the Bible and usually knew the reference.

'It's all there in 1 Corinthians 14 as well. Verses 33 to 36. Women should remain silent in church and be in submission.'

'But', said Edith, 'if that was taken literally there'd be

79

no sopranos or altos in the choir. And all these very biblical missionary societies allow women to preach and teach overseas, because the men just aren't there. I heard of a lady the other day who is a director or something in a Christian organization, but she isn't allowed to pray aloud in her own church. It's all ridiculous. Surely times have changed.'

'Yes, of course times have changed, but are we going to twist the Scriptures to adapt them to "the times"?'

'No, but we need to interpret them properly.'

'There you go, "interpretation, interpretation". I agree with Bob Renshaw, you know. I used to think he was a bad example to the church, but since I've got to know him I've realized that he's a man of Scripture. He says that "interpreting" the Bible nearly always means diluting it. I think he's right.'

'Let's ask Timothy,' said Edith. 'This question is really an extension of the family roles one that is being discussed in the house groups and will be in the church weekend. We've assumed that the question of leadership, male or female, was only about family: father, mother, children. But it goes beyond that into the family of the church. Whatever we say about Adam and Eve and the fall and Paul's letters applies to men and women in the church as well as at home.'

'More than that,' said Cyril, 'it applies to the state as well. Whether people are Christians or not, God's creation principles remain. If the man is supposed to be the head of his family, men should lead in the church and men should lead in the state.'

'What about the Queen?' said Edith.

'Well, I'll make an exception for the Queen' (Cyril was a loyal citizen), 'but we're better off with a man as Prime

80

Minister, I'll be bound.'

'I think you may be right,' said Edith placidly, ignoring Cyril's opening his eyes very widely, 'not that men should rule in everything, but that what applies to home should apply to church and to industry and government.'

'But you said that in the first place.'

'Yes dear, and you agreed. That's why I think you're probably right.'

Who do Adam and Eve stand for?

'I had a phone call from Cyril this afternoon.'

Timothy and Diana were taking baby Rebecca for a walk in the park, or rather Diana was, and Timothy had come as well.

'So *that's* who it was.' The phone call had kept Timothy away from their discussions with Sue, the prospective curate, for about fifteen minutes.

'Yes. I should have told him I'd ring back, but he said it was to be a very short call. It just seemed to go on. Anyway it gave you a chance to get to know Sue. She's nice, isn't she?'

'Yes, very nice,' said Diana, without enthusiasm. 'Too nice. She looks too much like Venus de Milo for my liking. If you had her as a colleague you'd never keep your mind on your work. You might as well have Sallie as a curate, but at least she has Nigel to look after her, I suppose.'

Timothy blushed despite his best efforts not to. Diana was well aware that he was an admirer of Sallie's face and form. He was also quick to concede the point.

'I suppose you may be right,' he said slowly. 'I think

that the lobby for women's ordination hasn't fully taken into account the temptation that a pretty woman can be for the men in the congregation, let alone the man she has to work with. Do you remember that Communion service in the Lutheran church that we went to on holiday? That woman minister. When she gave me the chalice she looked into my eyes. I nearly melted on the spot. I'm sure I thought much more of her than the Communion. Yes, you may be right.'

Diana could hardly contain herself. 'But,' she spluttered, 'if you think that this would be a problem for the men when a woman is ministering, why isn't it a problem for the *women* when men have been doing it all this time?'

'I'd never thought of that.'

'No, of course you hadn't. That's typical of men! Anyway I don't think anyone in our church has that problem with you. Oh dear, I wish I hadn't said that. I don't mean it, really.'

Here they were, arguing again. The interview with Sue had seemed a success, the rain had stopped, the sun had come out and a walk in the park should have been delightful. Now this.

'Let's talk about curates another time,' said Timothy. 'It's too nice an afternoon to spoil it by arguing.'

'Well then, what did Cyril say?'

'Oh, he was talking about women curates,' said Timothy with an attempt at a laugh.

'That was a coincidence.'

'Not really. Edith had directed Sue from the station, remember. She must have put two and two together and seen Sue as a possible curate.'

'Cyril wouldn't approve.'

'No. He wants to include women's ordination on the agenda for the house groups and the church weekend. *And* women in industry and government as well.'

'Help!' said Diana. 'There wouldn't be time.'

'That's what I told him,' said Timothy, 'but he was quite determined. It's an interesting point.'

'What is?'

'Well, he agreed that Adam and Eve represented man and wife, though he was very quick to assure me that they were not just symbolic characters, they were real people as well. Edith has been filling him in on the house group discussions – he's really well enough to get to a meeting himself now, you know, we must arrange for him to have transport – anyway he has put the question this way:

'"Who do Adam and Eve stand for?" They represent man and wife, so the fall spoils marriage relationships, husbands get bossy, wives get rebellious and all that. But then do Adam and Eve stand for religious people in general as well? That would mean that the original good relating in the Garden of Eden should be seen in our churches and that the fall has spoilt man/woman co-operation in church too.'

'And is Paul helping when he tells women to stay out of church matters altogether? I suppose he would have allowed them to make the tea.'

Timothy ignored this remark. 'But it goes further, doesn't it? Do Adam and Eve represent man- and womankind in all things, whether they are religious or not? In day-by-day living, in industry and commerce, in government and finance? Has the fall affected those relationships?'

'Of course it has.'

'Of course it has, yes. So it's totally inconsistent to say that a woman may have a career as a director of a chain of shops and, at the same time, deny her the chance to lead in church.'

'Yes.'

'She should be either free to do both and be equal with her husband, or, if the male really is the leader, she should be willing to take second place in all three spheres.'

'Yes, that makes sense.'

'So Cyril wants us to include all that in our studies.'

'Well, we could say what we've just said, but to explore all the arguments on both sides for women's ordination, women's careers and all that would require three separate courses at the very least.'

'Exactly,' said Timothy. 'I persuaded him that we might tackle one of them every other year.'

'What did he say?'

'He said that it would be literally over his dead body by the time we'd finished. Anyway I think we can say that whatever applies to marriage in the leadership equation also applies to church and state.'

'And vice versa?'

'What do you mean?'

'Proverbs 31 of course. The good wife there is in charge of the house and the family business. Her husband thinks that's great and lets her get on with it (perhaps he tried to stop her and couldn't). If he'd been a vicar, his wife would have been running his church for him as well.'

Baby Rebecca was not old enough to understand why her pram was suddenly propelled at great speed and why her mother was laughing, yes laughing, and why

her daddy was pretending to throw things after them.
But they arrived home feeling better than they had for
some months.

> **Do you think that Adam and Eve represent man
> and woman in general or only husband and wife?
> Do attractive ministers deflect worshippers'
> minds from God?
> How can this be allowed for?**

10

A single problem

Jane Goodrich marched resolutely across the pedestrian crossing to Canwell Park station, looking neither to the right nor the left. Her companion, Gina Renshaw, caught her up with an effort.

'For someone suffering from arthritis you don't do too badly,' she said cheerfully. 'I can hardly keep up with you.'

Jane was apologetic. 'The problem is that I can't bear to look at the Vicarage. Every time I come this way I have to scuttle past on the other side of the road.' Gina said nothing, but gave Jane's arm a squeeze.

Jane was still in the 'I can never forgive myself' stage after her escapade with baby Rebecca. Oh yes, the

Monteiths had been marvellously understanding and helpful. They hadn't taken the matter any further. They realized that Jane was under stress. Her doctor had been understanding, too. He had prescribed yet another course of new tablets. But that made her feel guilty too. At nearly sixty-six, here she was taking seven different kinds of pills. Her mother had died at the age of ninety-seven. How many pills would Jane be taking by that time?

The church had recognized Jane's problems and Gina, as a near neighbour, had been asked to look after her. Part of the treatment, in Gina's book, was a trip to the West End of London, to get away from Canwell Park for a day, treat themselves to a good lunch and spend some time window-shopping in Oxford Street.

Which was why Jane and Gina were to be found one Saturday morning, boarding the District Line train bound for Notting Hill Gate and thence to Oxford Circus.

A different world

During the journey Gina tried to engage Jane in conversation, in the hope of helping her to feel more positive. She told Jane about the house group meetings and the forthcoming family weekend. Jane was politely interested. She asked Jane about her own views on the subject, but Jane said she had none and couldn't think it likely that she ever would have.

After attempting to catch Jane's attention by talking about fashion, cooking, carpets, curtains and the terrible price of butter, and attempting in vain, Gina allowed silence to prevail. They changed trains at

Notting Hill Gate and were soon at Oxford Circus.

One of the experiences which modern life offers is the rapid exchange of one environment for another. The air-traveller can board the aircraft in sub-zero temperatures and alight a few hours later in the tropics. The television viewer can roam the world in imagination from the depths of an armchair. But there remains a unique sensation, which has been experienced now for nearly a hundred years by all those who travel by underground train to central London.

Suburban stations are faceless enough. Remove the name-boards and it would be difficult for travellers to know whether they were north or south of the Thames, east or west of the Metropolis. But there is a sense of *locality* about them. There are usually some trees to be seen, at least in the distance. You might see someone you know. There's a parish church, the newsagents, the row of houses, the petrol station. This is *home* to a few thousand people. They belong here. They can move about and recognize the friendly landmarks.

This friendly suburb, however, has a hole in it, a gateway to another world, a 'tube' down which thousands of Londoners are sucked every day. Walk down the half-deserted platform on a Saturday morning, choose a seat (this is the end of the line, so the trains are never full here on a Saturday), hear the doors slide shut and surrender yourself to half an hour of lurching and jolting and trying to understand the subtleties of the advertisements above your head.

Perhaps this process of shaking has an anaesthetizing effect, which means that all memory of the leafy suburb so recently left behind is erased, but when the doors open at Oxford Circus, the same sort of doors that you came in by so recently, you have surely entered a new world.

London slams into you, so that initially you lose your breath. Could there be any air left when all these people have finished breathing it? The buildings are ten times higher than the ones you left behind. The traffic is at a standstill (except when you try to cross the street, when it moves at astonishing speed) and you emerge from your hole in the ground to join a line of red buses and another line of black taxicabs. And the people! Huge slabs of people moving in opposite directions somehow miraculously get past each other without pitched battles.

And the noise! Traffic, aircraft and street vendors shouting their wares. It's deafening. And the smell! Petrol fumes and more petrol fumes. Inhale them if you dare. Breathe if you must.

The effect of all this on the Jane Goodriches of this world is devastating. People who are used to long nights of patient watching as elderly relatives demand their attention; for whom a visit to the supermarket is an adventure and an evening out at a church council meeting next door to paradise, such people do not enjoy Oxford Street on a Saturday morning.

The astonishing thing is that some people *do*. Gina almost leapt up the subway steps and swung round to meet Jane, as if welcoming her to a party.

'Come on Jane!' she cried, her excitement barely concealed. 'Where shall we go first?'

Jane responded with a shallow smile and, 'Anywhere you like, dear. It's ten years since I was here. All the shops have changed hands, I think.'

Her quiet voice was lost in the roar of London's

traffic, so Gina took her by the arm and steered her past a bewildering array of cavernous shop-fronts, mostly brightly lit and often emitting deafening pop music. A lot of them seemed to be dark green. The names flashed on lighted signs, 'Top Spot', 'The Leg Shop', 'Stocking Rack', 'Baby Boots', 'Bodies', 'Kowloon Moon' (this appeared to be a Chinese restaurant, but in fact seemed to be selling fortune-telling equipment), 'Hi Fi Sky', 'Sex 'n' sox' and so many more that Jane found it more restful to look at the traffic.

'I've got no-one'

Noticing that Jane appeared to be sleep-walking, Gina steered her into the nearest Pizza Post (which claimed to be able to post a Pizza to your home so quickly that it would arrive piping-hot through the letter box and at no more than six times the price of the product). They sat down beneath the dark green shade of a plastic palm tree, surrounded by dark green fences around the dark green table. After about half an hour's wait they were served with a huge circular pizza which Jane fully expected to be dark green.

Gina breathed in the atmosphere with delight and exchanged pleasantries with the waiter, who called himself Luigi but who seemed to have learnt his English within the sound of Bow Bells. She turned happily to ask Jane whether she was enjoying her pizza and saw to her dismay that Jane had put down her knife and fork and was quietly sobbing.

'Jane! My poor dear, whatever's the matter?' Gina was immediately alert to her companion's distress. 'I know you find London a bit bewildering, but it's not as bad as all that, is it?'

'No, it's not London, at least not really,' said Jane, at last recovering herself. 'It's just that all these shops selling wedding dresses and baby growbags' (Gina thought she had better let this one go unremarked in the present atmosphere) 'and, and people doing things together. It makes one feel so *lonely* and single. They all seem to have somebody and I've got no-one.'

'But you have got someone, there are plenty of us, Jane. That's the whole point of the family of the church. We are all brothers and sisters in Christ. We're an enormous family.'

'Yes, too enormous. It's all very well for you to talk like that, Gina, but the church family is not the same as a real flesh-and-blood family – someone to come home to. Oh yes, people are all very helpful if you telephone them and some people call occasionally for a chat, but they're not *there* with you.'

'I do know exactly what you feel like, Jane,' said Gina. 'Remember that I was on my own for a long time after Andrew, er, went.' (Gina's first husband, Andrew, to whom she had been devoted, had been killed in a road accident.)

'I suppose you do,' said Jane, not prepared to be comforted, 'but you're married again, so you do now have someone, don't you?'

'Yes, I do, but...'

'And all this business about the church study groups. They're discussing husbands and wives all the time. Then they have family services. Husbands, wives and children. What about us, the people who have no families?'

'But', said Gina, 'the family service is not just for

families to come to. It means a service for the family which is the church. And you're part of it.'

'It doesn't feel like that,' said Jane, near to tears again, 'and when they ask you out it feels as if they're pitying you. Oh dear, I don't mean that you're pitying me now. But you know what I'm getting at. And that family growth weekend sounds like more of the same thing.'

'Now listen, Jane, I do hear what you're saying and, whether you believe me or not, I have experienced something of what you're suffering. But do remember that you're only a few weeks into bereavement and that's a shock that puts people out of gear for ages. People have said how well you've taken your mother's death, but you mustn't try to take it too well. I mean, you need to grieve, you *need* to show emotion. And I'm glad you're able to now.'

'Your husband told me that I was self-pitying,' said Jane anxiously.

'My husband had no right to tell you that,' said Gina, colouring. 'If this were two years into the future and you were still in the same place, perhaps a bit of confrontation would be necessary. But not yet. In any case – well, you've probably guessed that Bob and I have our problems. We don't see things from the same angle. Sometimes, you know, it's easier to be single than to be married.'

'Oh Gina,' said Jane in alarm, 'I'm so sorry! Here have I been burdening you with all my problems and you've got problems of your own all the time.'

'Bless you, no. I think it was very good for you to talk as you have done. But look, let's at least finish these half-cold pizzas and then make some positive plans.'

'I think I can look at the Vicarage again'

At this point 'Luigi', with amazing perception, seeing that his customers had served themselves to half the pizza and had not eaten even those portions, insisted on bearing away the three plates and returning in less than five minutes with a steaming half-pizza, two fresh hot plates and two cups of coffee.

'Thanks, Luigi,' said Gina approvingly. 'We'll come here again.'

'That's what you're supposed to say, luv,' said Luigi and favoured her with a broad wink.

After a little more necessary shopping, to Jane's great relief they caught the train for home. On the way they decided on a plan of campaign. Gina would discuss with Timothy the idea of a 'drop in' open house meeting for married and especially single people, not necessarily to study or indulge in 'activities', but just as a mutual support and friendship group. Timothy was also to be reminded that Jane was now free from caring for her mother and, as her confidence gradually returned, she would be ready for some responsibility in the church ('future secretary of the "drop in fellowship",' said Gina to herself).

In return Jane promised to consider coming to the family growth weekend, on being assured that part of the programme was specifically geared to single people in the church.

The doors opened, the steps were climbed and the cool breeze of an October evening greeted Gina and Jane as they emerged on the familiar Station Road.

'Thank you so much, Gina,' said Jane, as they turned

for home. 'I can't say I enjoyed Oxford Street, but it's all done me a lot of good. And you must tell me how I can help *you*. I don't mean to interfere, but perhaps I can pray for you, anyway. And', she said, taking a deep breath, 'I think I can look at the Vicarage as we go past.'

How does your church/how do you, set about helping people who are bereaved?
How does your church/how do you, relate to single people?
If you are single, how do you relate to the rest?
How can the situation be improved?

—— 11 ——
Knights errant?

T he electric light rattled as a succession of thunderous bumps upstairs shook the house.

'What*ever* is going on?' Gordon Barber had just returned from a Saturday morning shopping expedition ('it's worse than Oxford Circus down there today!') and had sunk gratefully into an armchair.

'It's Shelley's boyfriend, Jason,' said Margaret sweetly.

'Shelley's *what*? Is he a coal merchant or something? And how long has she had a boyfriend? She's nine, isn't she?'

The room shook again, in response to another heavy impact from above. Gordon was never a man to let things happen about his head without knowing why or how. Forgetting his exhaustion, he leapt up the stairs and flung open Shelley's bedroom door. His first impression was of Shelley, dressed in a brightly-coloured sweatshirt, a short skirt and a pair of high-heeled shoes, which were too big for her and rather obviously her mother's. Her hair was scraped up behind and tied with a ribbon and she was standing on a chair.

'Jump!' she shrieked, just as Gordon opened the door.

There was another crash. As he pushed the door fully open Gordon beheld a heavy-looking boy of about eleven, collapsed in a heap on the floor. He looked up, reddened and appeared very confused.

'What*ever* is going on?' Gordon said again.

'This is Jason. He's my new boyfriend,' said Shelley.

'Hi Jason!' said Gordon weakly.

'Hello,' said the boyfriend, getting to his feet.

'Does your boyfriend have difficulty standing?' asked Gordon.

'He's jumping for me,' said Shelley happily. 'I told him he had to jump over the clothes-horse and he hasn't done it yet.'

'Why does he have to do that?'

'Because he's my boyfriend. That means he'll do whatever I tell him to. Won't you Jason?' Jason looked sheepish but did not deny it.

'I thought boyfriends looked after girls and loved them.'

'Oh yes,' said Shelley, 'he does love me, don't you Jason?'

Jason said nothing and looked even more sheepish.

'That's why he does what I tell him to. He loves me so

much. But he doesn't need to look after me. That's silly. I can look after myself.'

'Boys looked after girls when I was young.'

Shelley looked at her father with pity in her eyes. 'Perhaps they did in the olden days,' she said, 'but things are different now.'

'Well,' said Gordon, putting his hand to his head, 'they obviously are. But they've got to be different here, too, because I'm afraid you'll bring the ceiling down. I think you had better take your knight errant outside. It's stopped raining.'

'What's a knight errant?' asked Shelley, jumping off her chair.

'The young man in the Middle Ages, who went about doing brave deeds to delight his lady-love.'

'Was that before you were young, Daddy?'

'Outside!' said Gordon, and the question was never answered.

Birds jumping up and down

'This world is upside down,' said Gordon, restored now to his armchair and gratefully accepting the cup of mid-morning coffee which Margaret offered him. 'Father does the shopping and daughter has a boyfriend at the age of nine and apparently he promises to love and obey *her*.'

'But I made the coffee.'

'Yes, dear, thank you, I'm grateful for that. But what do you think about Shelley and her boyfriend?'

'I think they're going through a perfectly normal phase of growing up. They pick up all this romantic love stuff from pop songs and try to copy it. They're too young as yet to feel the sexual attraction but they're going through gender-role games, expressing the differences between the sexes that are becoming clearer.'

'Um. That sounds very plausible,' said Gordon thoughtfully. 'But I thought modern life was supposed to destroy the differences between the sexes. I thought they were supposed to be exactly equal. What seems to be happening here is a violent reversal of the roles. Previously woman obeyed man, now man obeys woman. Where do they get that from?'

'Well, it's not new, is it? You mentioned the knight errant business. The chivalry of the Middle Ages was all about men doing spectacular things to impress women.'

'Yes,' said Gordon, 'but it was because they were chivalrous. They didn't have to do those things. It was because they loved their ladies.'

'Nonsense!' said his wife cheerfully. 'They were trying to impress them. The men were competing with each other to decide who would win the lady's hand. If they didn't actually fight over it, it was a question of who could do the most spectacular deeds. You see it in the male animal, displaying all his ferocity, and the male bird, putting on bright colours and fluffing out his feathers and jumping up and down. The male usually succeeds in making himself look ridiculous. It makes me wonder why they do it. And the female must see through it all and despise him.'

Gordon was beginning to feel uncomfortable.

'Not really,' he said defensively, 'the male knows full well that these are foolish things to do, like the heroes of the old legends slaughtering a few giants or the birds making themselves look silly or Jason jumping over the clothes-horse. The male has to do that sort of thing because it's the only way to impress the small female mind.'

'Now that really is chauvinist,' said Margaret. 'Scratch the balanced male and you find a chauvinist just beneath the surface.'

'Scratch the balanced female and you find a feminist just beneath the surface, who makes generalized remarks like that one.'

'In other words,' said Margaret, 'we're back to Genesis chapter 3 again. The relationships have gone wrong.'

'So, rather than argue one side's case or the other, the most positive thing to do is to ask how to improve the situation.'

Back to basics

'Well, where do we start?' asked Margaret. 'You're good at going back to basics. I'll chip in with the details. Perhaps that's a male/female distinction to start with.'

'Perhaps it is,' said Gordon, 'but don't let's get side-tracked before we've begun. The basic questions are, "Are men and women different?" If so, apart from the obvious physical differences, "What differences should we emphasize and encourage and what differences should we try to eliminate?"'

'OK, then, what are the facts?'

'This is where the trouble starts,' said Gordon. 'Men and women have different bodies and different roles in producing children. And on average women tend to be smaller than men and not quite so physically strong.

Having said that, the facts are hard to come by.'

'But surely lots of tests have been done to see whether boys are better than girls at maths or sewing and all that.'

'Yes, they have, but I can't see that they prove very much. The obvious problem is that if, for instance, boys tend to be better than girls at technical drawing, it may be because they have been brought up to consider themselves "technically minded" and girls have been encouraged to think of themselves as the opposite. Equal opportunities in schools and general open discussion of the matter will not remove the very deep-seated female ideal of the gentle home-maker who is good at languages, arts subjects and cookery, while the male is the hunter, gatherer, scientist, technician and coal-heaver, not if those ideas have been around in the home from the very earliest days of the child's life.'

'But what we need to know is, are those natural characteristics so that men and women really function better in those roles, or are they merely pushed that way by centuries of prejudice?'

'Exactly. They might have become "natural" because of the very long time they have been assumed to be true. But did God intend them to be like that originally? The old rhyme said, "When Adam delved and Eve span, who then was the gentleman?" But that was an argument for the equal status of high and low in society. Unwittingly they imported some fourteenth-century assumptions about the Garden of Eden. The Bible doesn't say that Adam did the digging and Eve the spinning. In fact they had no need of spinning anyway. All we know is that God made them in his image and told them jointly to be good stewards of the world.'

Margaret sighed. 'But these are not facts,' she said. 'What about these experiments? You've read books, haven't you?'

'Yes, one or two. But, as I said, there are problems. As far as possible the experiments allow for the possible conditioning of upbringing and the environment and when they have done that well, they seem to suggest that boys and girls, women and men are generally equal in ability in nearly every area. But...'

'There would be a "but".'

'Yes. But the interpretation of the "facts" is usually done by either a man or woman...'

'You surprise me,' said Margaret.

'Who is to some degree interested in showing either that one sex is superior or that both are equal. So the "facts" are interpreted for us and become arguments rather than facts. The best book I've read recently was by a woman. But, however scientific she's being, she's *glad* to discover experiments which show equality. It's very difficult.'

'Back to square one'

'So we can never know the answer?'

'No, what I'm saying is that men and women are near enough equal in everything except muscle and child-bearing and that we shall never find out *scientifically* whether they have particular roles to play. We need to go back to what feels comfortable, what our own society expects and, for the Christian, what the Bible has to say.'

'Back to square one, then.'

'Well, not quite. What I would argue for is *choice*. In Christ there is neither male nor female (Galatians

3:28). I expect that means that God does not prefer men to women, as the ancient Jews assumed that he did. But perhaps it also means that the old barriers are not as solid as we thought. They can be broken down. If, in Christ, a man is called to cook, wash and sew, then he should exercise his gifts in that way. If a woman is called to manage a factory or a football team, her sex need not debar her. What is wrong is when society or a part of society insists on making roles for other people.'

'And the difference between the sexes?'

'Well, as you know, I think that the difference should be emphasized. We have so much richness to bring to one another as men and women. It would be so sad to be all middle-sex. A gifted chef will cook as well as any woman but he brings a male approach to it. A woman manager should do the job as a female and not be expected to do the job as if she were a man.'

'And women ministers?'

The question was not answered that day. Gordon had noticed a violent shaking of his hawthorn hedge and had shot out of his chair to investigate. He discovered a dishevelled Jason, bleeding from several fresh scratches, emerging from the hedge.

'He did it for *me*,' simpered Shelley.

Gordon groaned.

Do men and women have 'naturally different' roles to play in life?

Should individuals be left to decide on their own? Can you think of situations where that choice might spoil a family, a church, a club? Would it matter?

12
Shoes, hats and headship

'We were going to think a bit more about what you said when Nigel and Sallie were here,' said Margaret, after Jason's wounds had been attended to. 'You know, the problem of coming to the Bible from a preconceived angle and reading out of it what you want. It's rather like this business of seeing male and female roles according to current fashions.'

'What's Shelley doing this afternoon?' asked Gordon.

'Going to Jason's for tea.'

'She'll probably make him pour out tea for her while kneeling in adoration. Anyway, that's good. We could go for a walk and carry on our discussion then.'

'I wonder if Nigel and Sallie could come.'

A telephone call revealed that Nigel and Sallie would be busy until the middle of the afternoon, but a meeting-place was arranged for three o'clock. As soon as Shelley had departed for her beloved's castle Gordon and Margaret opened the little gate which led from their back garden into the park. The autumn orange and gold on the trees was at its best and the still-warm sunshine greeted the Barbers with an immediate sense of well-being.

'It's only a few weeks since that terrible "Vicar's voyage" when we had the thunderstorm,' said Gordon. 'It seems like a year. A lot has happened since then.'

'But this is a much better day for a walk,' said his wife, taking his hand.

A key to unlock the Bible?

'Where did we get to?'

'We started to work out how we could read the Bible', said Gordon, 'without distorting it.'

'So what are the main ways of distorting it? I can think of two straight away; reading out of the Bible what you want, rather than what it says, and reading what you don't want.'

'Explain,' said Gordon.

'Well, in the first place the danger is that we come to the Bible with our minds made up and find justification for our prejudices. This is what we talked about before. If I want to prove that women and men are equal, I find all the verses that say that and explain away the ones that don't.'

'Yes,' said Gordon, 'and because it's the Bible we're talking about we have the added danger of underlining our prejudices by saying "God's Word says it, too", or "the Lord spoke to me this way". We come to the Bible to confirm our wishes, not to find wisdom that will guide us. But why reading what you *don't* want?'

'That's the equal and opposite reaction. Lots of people with tender consciences and a negative view of things assume that the Bible will tell them "thou shalt not". They come to it in fear and dread and as soon as their eyes light on some warning or hint of judgment they say, "I thought so" and give up. People who regard God with fear as a secret police officer in the sky, waiting to pounce on any little fault, find him to be like that in their Bible.'

'But', said Gordon, 'it's the same Bible for the optimist who sees God as a heavenly Father on every page.'

'Exactly. You can read out of it what you *want* or *fear* to find, but miss what it really says. The person who has had a peaceful family upbringing with a kind father will usually see God as kind and just. The person with a broken home and a drunken father who beats his wife will see God in that light, too, not always but often. And even the children whose father died when they were little may pin their resentments on God.'

They reached the end of the park at this point, crossed over Highwood Avenue, took the path beside the school and made for Canford Heath, a wide area of common land, dotted with trees and bushes and today, as usual, well provided with dogs and their owners, taking each other for walks.

'And, I suppose, under this heading,' said Margaret, as they returned to an easy pace after crossing the road, 'comes the problem we were talking about at the group meeting, interpreting the Bible according to the fashions of the day, so the people who assumed that men were superior to women saw all of it in the Bible and nowadays many people see the opposite.'

'Yes,' said Gordon. 'It even comes out a bit in the translation. I noticed that the old versions of 1 Timothy 2:12 say that Paul will not permit women to "usurp" authority over men. The modern versions tone it down a bit and say "have" authority. We can't help bringing our own world-view with us.

'In fact some people think that each age has to have its own key to unlock the meaning of the Bible – so it means something different for each generation according to their needs.'

'That sounds dangerous.'

'Yes it does, because it means, *a.* that the Bible cannot be fully understood by the ordinary person without having learnt what the key is – you know the old simple ploughboy knowing more of the Bible than a learned professor. Wasn't it Tyndale who said that?'

'And *b.*?'

'And *b.* that the Bible means something different for each generation, so it is no longer a source of revelation but a sort of mirror, reflecting back the needs of the age. It means that the Bible truth is only relative. It changes. It is not God's definitive message.'

'So what hope have we of ever understanding what that message is, if there are so many things in the way? And what can we say to Nigel and Sallie? We're due to meet them in less than half an hour.'

'There's more to come,' said Gordon brightly. 'What about bare feet in church?'

106

Bare feet in church

'Go on, then,' said Margaret, 'what about bare feet in church?'

'I mean all this business about culture. Do we take at face value every detail of what the Bible says because it's God's Word, or do we apply the principles in modern terms? The old chestnut is women wearing hats in church. We don't usually follow that, because the *significance* of wearing hats has changed. It may be that the bareheaded woman in Paul's day was a loose woman.'

'But some people still insist on women wearing hats in church. Some churches still do.'

'Exactly, but they are being inconsistent if the men do not take off their shoes to worship. The same Bible says both. God told Moses to take off his shoes because he was in God's presence at the burning bush. So we pick and choose. We obey some commands literally and ignore others.

'More to the point of our discussion, Paul says that women should be silent in church and that they should not teach. That's in 2 Timothy 2 as well. By one means or another those injunctions are ignored in most churches today. We say, "the women were chattering during the service, so Paul was asking for discipline." Or "you wouldn't *expect* women to teach men in those days. It was unthinkable." At least it must have been thought of or Paul wouldn't have forbidden it, but we are happy to say, "Things have changed now. The principle behind what Paul was saying is that those who teach ought to be those who are fitted for teaching. Women couldn't be then, because they couldn't read or write, of course. They often are now." So women teach in Sunday school, lead missionary programmes, preach and minister.'

'Hey, wait a minute,' said Margaret, stopping short to watch a grey squirrel scampering across the path and up the trunk of a beech tree. 'Where does the headship argument fit into all this? I mean, if we say that women may teach and preach in church because men no longer have the authority they did in Paul's time, then the same argument must apply to husbands and wives. Men no longer have the authority they did, so we should argue that the leader should be the one best fitted for leadership, in Paul's day inevitably the male, but today it could be either.'

'Well, that's the logic of it,' said Gordon. 'Yes. We are being inconsistent if we hold to male headship "because the Bible says so" but ignore the hat-wearing and bare feet and women teaching on the grounds of cultural change. There they are!'

This last ejaculation signalled the appearance in the distance of Nigel and Sallie, making for the appointed meeting-place, a small spinney of Scots pines at the highest point of the Heath, from which one could see central London on a good day.

'Is that any clearer?'

The two couples greeted each other joyfully and made the usual remarks about the weather and why you couldn't see St Paul's Cathedral today and was pollution getting worse?

'Right, then,' said Nigel, 'what conclusions have you come to?'

'What indeed?' said Margaret archly.

So Gordon explained, with frequent interruptions from his wife, where their discussions had led them so far.

'What I think I hear you saying, then,' said Sallie slowly, 'is that the truth is there in the Bible right enough. But the problem is with us. We come to it from the wrong angle, so we don't always get the right message.'

'Yes.'

'And that wrong angle may be caused by our upbringing, our present cultural fashions, our wilful misunderstanding, our lack of knowledge of historical customs or our lack of knowing precisely how to interpret the Bible.'

'Yees.'

'So, on the one hand, the Bible is as clear as daylight and the simple ploughboy or car-park attendant can, with the help of God's Spirit, understand the truth.'

'Yeees.'

'But on the other hand, to understand the truth you need a vast array of learned psychological, philosophical, historical and interpretative tricks. In other words, keys!'

'Who's swallowed a dictionary?' said Nigel, secretly impressed by this display of long words from his wife.

'Never mind that,' said Sallie. 'Which is right? Is the Bible clear on its own, without all these keys, in which case the ploughboy picking up Paul's letters will learn that wives must submit to their husbands and women must not speak in church. Or do we need all the keys, in which case only a few clever people will be able to understand it all?'

109

'You've just summarized the sixteenth-century debate on private interpretation,' said Gordon.

'Who's swallowed a history book?' said Sallie.

'Well, the Roman Catholic church said that the Bible needed careful interpretation. The priests were trained to do it and the ordinary people were forbidden to read it in case they got it wrong. The Reformation came along and said that God's Word was clear to anyone, so Luther translated the Bible into German, Tyndale into English, and people began to learn to read so that they could read the Bible for themselves. Printing meant that copies could be made available.'

'That's the history lesson, dear,' said Margaret, 'but which of them was right?'

Gordon paused for a moment, just long enough for his three companions to exchange glances. All four chorussed together:

'They both were!'

Several nearby dogs and their owners looked up in surprise at this unwonted disturbance of the Saturday-afternoon peace and the two couples were reduced to helpless mirth. Gordon always managed to conclude discussion on apparently contradictory arguments by agreeing with both sides.

'Is that any clearer?' he said after a while. 'The point is that the more we understand our own weaknesses and allow for them, the better we shall understand the message of the Bible. So those who are good at Bible interpretation ought to help those who are not. But that doesn't prevent our ploughboy from learning the message with the Holy Spirit's help. Though he might get it wrong more often than the gifted interpreter. He should go to his church, where people can help each

110

other to hear clearly.'

'Which is all a plug for St Barnabas' and the Sunday morning sermon, I suppose,' said Nigel, 'or is that the sixteenth-century Catholic view?'

'Both, probably,' said Sallie.

Have you had the experience of God speaking to you through the Bible?

Have you had that experience and found later that you were mistaken? Did you admit it?

How can you improve your listening skills?

13

'I'm not upset!'

'**I**'m still waiting,' said Diana Monteith, holding Rebecca on one arm and pouring out tea with the other hand, 'for an answer about slavery.'

'Mm?' said Timothy, who also had both hands full, one with a slice of toast and marmalade and the other with the daily paper.

'You know, Paul said slaves should obey masters and wives should obey husbands. We've abolished slavery in the factory and are trying to keep it in the home.'

Wearily Timothy laid down the paper.

'We haven't time to discuss it *now*,' he said. 'I have to be in London for ten o'clock. Won't it wait?'

'You could read the paper on the train,' said Diana

firmly. 'You never seem to have time nowadays if it's a question of talking to me. You have plenty of time to go to meetings or read newspapers.'

Timothy obediently folded his paper and racked his brains for an answer to the question, which, in the business of the past few days, he had forgotten.

'All right, then,' he said at last, 'I remember the point now. You argued that slavery has been abolished, mainly through Christian influence, and we all approve, so we disregard Peter's command, "slaves, obey your masters," because there are no more slaves. But you want to say that equality of the sexes is now an established fact too, so we must disregard Peter's command, "wives, obey your husbands." Is that right?'

'Yes.'

'Well, there's a big fallacy straight away.'

'Which is?'

'There are no slaves, in our society at least, but there *are* husbands and wives. Slavery has been abolished, but marriage hasn't.'

'That, from a man, is totally illogical,' said Diana.

Timothy groaned inwardly. He shouldn't have been drawn into this in the first place. Morning was never his best time. And Diana always seemed to want an argument. Here she was dragging sexist jargon into it as well, 'that, from a man'! The trouble was that he had an unpleasant feeling that she was right and that made him feel even more defensive.

Factor x

'What I am saying is that slavery has been abolished,' Diana continued, 'as a bad relationship between boss

113

and employee. Bosses and employees haven't been abolished. But their relationship has been improved. If "wives, obey your husbands" is followed we still have a bad old relationship between the sexes, and call it God's will, while God's will seems to have been reversed where workers are concerned.'

'Yes,' said Timothy, 'but God never intended slavery. It's not in the plan at the beginning. It was one of the results of the fall.'

'So was the headship of the male, according to your argument the other week.'

Timothy's brain was becoming clearer. It was the word 'headship' that reminded him.

'No,' he said firmly, 'I never said that the headship of the husband was the result of the fall. It was the *tyranny* of the husband that was the result of the fall: headship sinfully exercised, twisted and selfish. In fact you may be right about the similarity between employer and employee and husband and wife ...'

'I didn't say that you *employed* me! That's a typical male argument, that is.'

'Now let me finish what I was saying. I didn't mean that husbands employ wives. This is how it looks to me:

'God's intention in the beginning was that there should be a perfect relationship between men and women, husbands and wives. I don't know exactly what that relationship was in the Garden of Eden, we are not told, but let's call it "factor x", to avoid any sexist feeling.

'Factor x, the perfect relationship, was an equal relationship but not identical. Husband related to wife differently from wife to husband. There was a rich complementarity. But "factor x" was shattered at the

114

fall and became dominance and servility.

'There weren't any bosses and employees in the Garden of Eden, but God must surely have wished a perfect relationship between those who direct and those who co-operate in the directing. Adam and Eve were equally stewards of the Garden. The fall ensured that all that would go wrong, and slavery ensued. The intention is that "factor y" should exist between them. "Bosses" and "employees" should be equal, made in the image of God, but with different functions.

'Now I'm not saying,' said Timothy quickly, as he saw Diana taking a deep breath to interrupt, 'that factors x and y are the same. I don't mean to say that husbands should employ wives to carry out their instructions. But that is how it worked out through the centuries and that is how things were in the time when Paul was writing. And to some extent he was reflecting conditions as they were then. But he was also reflecting factor x in the context of things as they were then. If he were writing today he would express things rather differently, but he would still be expressing the same principle.

'The abolition of slavery has improved that aspect of working relationships, but it hasn't restored them to factor y, God's perfect plan. Perhaps that cannot be achieved in a fallen world. And so, the emancipation of women has improved things a lot but it hasn't, and cannot, restore the pre-fall factor x relationship. The question then is, "has the cross of Christ made that perfect relationship possible again?"'

'You never used to ...'

'Before you confuse the issue with talk about the cross, which always clinches every argument for you,' said Diana, 'I think I can still see your chauvinism showing through. What you said sounds very sensible and rational, but I notice that you said you didn't mean that husbands employ wives. Why didn't you think it possible that wives might employ husbands? It seems to me that your "factor x" is male headship by the back door all over again. Paul was right all along (he just used slightly different words from ours) and husbands rule OK.'

'I think you're deliberately trying to misunderstand what I'm saying,' said Timothy rather severely.

'And I think you're trying to make a reasoned defence for an unreasonable position.'

'Why is it,' said Timothy, 'that you have changed so much in the last few months? You never used to be so feminist. It's all changed since Becky was born. Don't you think some of these ideas are the result of your depression? It's not your fault, you know. It's like a broken leg. It will mend, given time.'

The look on Diana's face told Timothy at once that he should not have said this.

'How dare you be so condescending,' she said, 'as to pity me for my ideas just because they don't agree with yours!'

'I don't pity ...'

'Yes, you do. It's the typical male all over again. If you can't win your argument you attribute the opposing ideas to depression. Don't you see that you're devaluing me? I'm not supposed to be capable

116

of having reasonable ideas. Oh no. As soon as I have a reasonable idea it's because I'm emotionally disturbed. If you have a reasonable idea it's because it's biblical and rational. Well, I've had enough. Your ideas are not biblical and rational at all. They're all prompted by male chauvinism. But I don't blame you for it. You can't help it. It's like a broken leg. It will heal, given time.'

'This is impossible,' said Timothy. 'We can't have any kind of discussion on these terms.'

'You're right, and whose fault is it?'

'Well,' said Timothy as mildly as he could, 'you *are* a bit upset, you know.'

'I'm *not* upset,' shouted Diana and burst into tears.

'That woman'

By the time Timothy had tried, and failed, to comfort his wife and persuaded her to put Rebecca in her cot, since she had reacted to the atmosphere and was wailing pitifully, he realized that he would be late for his meeting in London. What was he to do? Was this a kind of emotional blackmail to keep him from his meeting, or did his duty lie in comforting a wife who was determined not to be comforted? Finally he said, 'I must go soon, darling. I shall be late for the meeting as it is.'

'Don't call me darling,' Diana sniffed. 'What meeting is it, anyway? I suppose *she*'ll be there?'

'She?' said Timothy innocently.

'Yes, that woman. What's her name, Susan, your pin-up girl.'

'I suppose she'll be there, yes, but that's not why I'm

going to the meeting.'

'No, I dare say,' said Diana cuttingly. 'That's not why you've been to a lot of meetings recently that she happens to be at as well. Perhaps you don't go because she's there, but it does make the meeting more pleasant for you, doesn't it? It's the old story. A man gets fed up with his wife when she's not well. When she's hale and hearty he's all monogamous and loving, but as soon as she has some depression he starts looking elsewhere for comfort. And she's just the right sort of understanding person. I expect she listens to your problems and offers to pray with you about them. She probably even agrees with you about male headship. What do you think all that does for *me*? It doesn't help much, does it?'

Timothy decided that further argument would be useless, so he kissed Diana's forehead and made for the station. He needed time to work this one out. Of course there was nothing between him and Sue, that was ridiculous. But then he had to admit it to himself that he was glad that she would be there. He did feel a security in her presence and she did seem to care for his problems. And she was uncommonly good-looking.

'O Lord,' said Timothy under his breath, 'why have you allowed me to get into this mess?'

'But then, I suppose I'm not really in a mess, yet,' he thought as he bought his ticket. 'I suppose I need to take the warning. But perhaps God has put Sue there just for such a time as this to help me over the problem. I'm sure she'll understand about this morning's scene. She'll listen patiently to it all. She's a very good listener. Perhaps we'll have lunch together again. There's no harm in that, surely. I need help at the moment. God knows that.'

To his intense disappointment, Sue was not at the meeting.

'Gordon here'

A succession of telephone calls had plundered the Barbers' evening. They had just decided that it was time to unplug the receiver and retire to bed when it rang yet again. Margaret was at first very annoyed, but, as she heard the concern in Gordon's voice, she realized that something serious was happening.

'Gordon here, yes... yes of course, why not?... no, it's not too late... really...oh, I'm sorry to hear that...*really*...yes of course, if you think we can help...both of you or just you?...yes, as soon as you like. It's better not to leave these things...yes, don't worry about it more than you must. We shall certainly pray for you, you know that...every blessing...'bye.'

'Who was that?' said Margaret, 'Gina or Bob?'

'Timothy,' said Gordon. 'Timothy and Diana.'

'Oh *no*,' said Margaret, 'whoever next?'

Do you think that slavery and husband-wife relationships were thought of similarly in Peter and Paul's time?

Has the situation changed radically for both today?

Do you find it hard to discuss things with someone you are emotionally involved with or a member of your family?

How do you cope with the problem?

14

'Yes, but...'

Three weeks later Gordon and Margaret were comparing notes. Gordon had had two meetings with Timothy and Margaret had just completed a second round of discussion with Diana.

'One thing is very positive,' said Gordon. 'At least they're both willing to talk about their problems. So many people, especially clergy, feel that they ought not to have problems at all and they're so ashamed of themselves that they never share their difficulties with anyone.'

'Yes,' said Margaret, 'but they're taking quite a risk in asking *us* to help them. I mean, members of their own church. It might have been better if they had found someone outside, someone none of us knew.'

'Well, it's a sign of their confidence in us. But I do agree that it's a big responsibility. We've got to be very careful that we don't betray their confidences. Very few people in the church suspect that they have problems.'

'Nigel and Sallie do.'

'Yes, and they are the people we have most to do with. I mean we are already discussing with them different couples' approaches to their problems. We shall have to find some way of keeping Tim and Diana out of the discussion now.'

'She's fighting all the time'

'So, how did you get on with Diana today?' Gordon stretched out his legs in front of the living-room gas fire.

'Rather "yes, but" again.'

'Meaning?'

'Well, we seem to be making some progress and affirm something definite, and when I say what I think we have agreed she will say "Yes, but ..."'

'For instance?'

'We had a good example of it this afternoon. I've been trying to help her to unload some of her negative feelings about the birth of Rebecca, her depression and then the trauma of Jane's little adventure, trying to help her to come to terms with the fact that she's not really well yet and that it isn't her fault. She's finding it very difficult to admit that she's not well anyway. She feels that all her defences against Timothy will collapse if she does. "He'll be proved right and I'll be proved wrong." Anyway, we've made some progress and she has admitted that she has been suffering from depression, so that's a good start.

'So I said, "We can agree as a baseline that you have been depressed, Diana." And she said, "Yes, but that doesn't mean that I'm wrong about what the Bible says about male domination and that Timothy's right."'

'She's fighting all the time, isn't she?'

'That's right,' said Margaret, 'she can't let go. She's fighting Timothy, the church, herself, Rebecca (she both adores and resents Rebecca). She's fighting me and I think she's fighting God. It's no use telling her that there's no need to fight. Nobody is against her, we're all on her side. She just has this drive inside her to fight. What we need to do is to help her to identify what it is that she's resenting, really. It may be something from long ago that she's buried and the results of it are coming out now. It's not straightforward ...'

'Will depressions ever be straightforward?' asked Gordon.

'Of course not,' said Margaret sadly, 'but the big complication here is the confusion between the depression, her relationship with Timothy and all this discussion about husband/wife relationships. It's almost impossible to disentangle the three. Almost any problem in the home can be blamed on Timothy and his thoughtlessness or on the Bible and its notions of male headship. If she admits to depression, then it must be someone else's fault if it isn't her own.'

'So discussion about what the Bible says is useless at this stage, I suppose,' said Gordon.

'Oh yes. She might agree to an interpretation of a verse of Scripture as being true and binding, but she will still say, "Yes, but" and find an ingenious way round it. What is really driving her is her emotional confusion. Timothy has told her that, which of course makes things much worse. He's not gifted with too much tact.'

'I think he knows it's wrong,' said Gordon, 'but he gets driven to desperation sometimes. He's human too, you know; he fights back. He needs as much help as Diana does. I think he's surviving all this remarkably well, but it's ironical that it should all blow up just when he's set the church on the track of exploring the husband/wife relationship. Just when he's asking us all to stand back from our emotions and understand clearly how to interpret the Bible, their own relationships are being driven by quite different motives.

'Even if we can all agree on the truth of a Bible doctrine, there's still a long way to go before we can put it into practice. It's hard enough to understand together what the right way is, but there are masses of obstacles in the way then to prevent us from actually *doing* anything right.'

Two impossible demands

'Yes. I've had another example of that only this week,' said Margaret. 'I was going to tell you. I met Gina in the doctor's surgery and she seemed to want to talk, so I waited for her and she called in for coffee on her way home. She'd only just gone when you came home. That was Wednesday you see.'

Gordon did see and he laughed ruefully. Wednesday had been the day of a dramatic homecoming. He had been anxious to get home early and had walked briskly and half-jogged from the station. As he burst through the garden gate he had stepped on wet leaves ('I told you, Gordon, you should have swept them up last week') and fallen heavily. He was still stiff and bruised and had a plaster on the side of his face. His accident had driven all thoughts of Gina's visit from Margaret's mind.

'Anyway, she told me how she and Bob have been getting on with the house groups and the studies. It seems as though they've been having quite a powerful effect on Bob. Although he wouldn't admit it, that episode when old Mrs Goodrich died really shook him up. I think he realized then that there were limits to male leadership, some things that he, at least, couldn't do as well as Gina. He's been arguing every step of the way, but he seems to have been greatly helped by his house group (it was a stroke of genius to separate him from Gina in the groups!).'

Gordon nodded happily. He had been responsible for the division of people into the groups.

'So, Gina says, they're getting on rather better at home. He has not abandoned his view of male headship, but he's happy now to accept the fact that Gina has gifts that he doesn't have and he's willing for her to exercise them. He's apparently quite proud of her because she's leading a group so well and he gets a bit of the reflected glory.

'But, and now I come to the point, he still goes on acting in a high-handed way, even though he agrees that they have a proper equality. Did you know that he'd been dragging her off to the 'Auld Alliance' every week to watch him play dominoes? You can imagine how much she enjoys that.'

'So that's where they go. I've seen them going down

the Avenue on Thursdays.'

'Well, he still says he knows what's best for her.'

'How does he justify that?'

'Gina told me.' And Margaret described Gina's discussion with Bob concerning the duties of husbands to love their wives and wives to submit to their husbands; how they had agreed that the husband's task was just as great as the wife's, that both were impossible but that they should aim towards the perfection; and how Bob had interpreted his duty to love his wife in a rather odd way.

'But he still goes on dragging Gina off to the "Alliance"?'

'Yes. He says that his love for Gina is so great that it's his duty to help her to submit to him. So instead of leaving her happily at home he makes her go with him.'

'I don't know whether to laugh or cry,' said Gordon.

'Cry, I think,' said Margaret. 'His real reason for taking her is probably to show her off to his mates. So he's justifying his actions by quoting Scripture to fit his own ideas.'

'Oh dear, don't we all,' said Gordon. 'I think we'd better change the subject or we shall be in danger of falling into the trap ourselves. We've talked enough for one day, anyway.'

No with a capital N

'I won't!' shrieked the child's voice.

'You jolly well will!' bellowed a male voice in response. There followed sounds of running footsteps and the slamming of a door. The windows rattled.

Nigel Rogers stared rather uncomfortably round the

neighbourhood and pretended not to have heard. He had rung the Barbers' doorbell twice, but there was obviously some problem between Gordon and young Shelley which had taken precedence over his approach. At last Gordon came to the door.

'So sorry to keep you, Nigel. Do come in. A little local difficulty. You heard it I expect. Girls seem to get adolescent at the age of nine nowadays. Do come in.'

Gordon looked harassed. In fact, as they walked into the brighter light of the sitting-room, Nigel thought that he looked positively grey.

'I'm sorry Margaret's not here,' said Gordon apologetically. 'She's completely washed out. She's gone to bed. She fainted this afternoon.'

'Fainted?'

'Yes, she's been overdoing it recently.'

'Without being too brutally frank, I must say that you don't look too good yourself,' said Nigel. 'What's been happening? Is there anything we can do to help?'

So Gordon told Nigel that they were trying to help several couples with their marriage problems, without telling him who they were, listening to Jane and her difficulties, trying to cope with a nearly adolescent daughter, and organizing the groups for the forthcoming family enrichment weekend, as well as being chiefly responsible for raising the balance of a third of a million pounds for the church rebuilding fund, oh and working as an accountant in the City five days a week.

Nigel made suitable sorry noises and received the leaflets he had come for regarding the family weekend. As he left he said,

'Do remember to call on us for anything we can do to help. It seems tragic to me that people like you with so

126

much to offer should drive yourselves too far. You know, between you, you can do an enormous range of things, yet one of the most important you don't seem to be able to do at all.'

'What's that?' asked Gordon nervously.

'Say "no" with a capital N,' said Nigel. 'Next time someone asks for help, try it. It works wonders.'

Why is it so difficult to translate good intentions and beliefs into good attitudes and actions?

How do you interpret Paul's injunctions to submit and love today?

Can you say 'No' when you should?

15

Somerton Court

T he car seemed to be alone in a universe consisting of nothing but fog. The headlights penetrated nothing, but the light was flung back from a wall of whiteness which seemed to begin a few feet in front of them. Jane Goodrich sincerely wished that she had not agreed to attend the family enrichment weekend. It had been hard enough to make the initial decision to go, harder still to leave her warm home on this late November afternoon, and here she was in little short of an agony of apprehension, in the back seat of Gordon's car with Bob and Gina Renshaw. Margaret sat tensely in the front seat making occasional nervous remarks like, 'We should be at Cross Gates by now' or, 'You're too close to the kerb' or, 'He didn't have his fog light on' and Gordon responded to each with a grunt.

In the back Gina, Bob and Jane remained silent, probably praying and gripping tightly whatever they could hold for security.

Gordon broke his silence. 'It's freezing now,' he said. This was worse than ever. He could hardly see anyway.

The journey seemed interminable. It was only forty-seven miles to Somerton Court. *Only*! They had already been on the road for two hours. At four, when they had left Canwell Park, there had still been some murky light, but that had soon given way to darkness. Gordon seemed to be plunging into the fog at reckless speed, yet the speedometer rarely moved above 20. Jane closed her eyes in despair. She caught herself praying that, if they must have an accident, at least they would all be killed instantly. This was dreadful. Whatever made such ideas grow? Where was the cheerful faith she used to have years ago? Years ago. She remembered what it was like to be a teenager, before the war. Which war? That was World War 2. The sun always shone in those days and there were bright starlit nights. Life was exciting and fresh and new ... Jane fell uneasily asleep.

Loving care

A rush of cold, sharp air awakened her. She started violently. The accident. It had happened! But it didn't look like an accident. Her door had been opened opposite a wide Gothic porch from which light was streaming. Gordon was cheerfully offering his arm to help her out. Diana and Timothy were there, silhouetted against the light.

'Jane! and Gina and Bob! What a relief to see you! No, you're not the last. And you haven't missed supper. It's all been put back an hour, so you've got time to settle in first.'

Oh, the bliss of that arrival! The richly panelled hall had an enormous fireplace full of sweet-smelling logs ablaze with welcome. There was a deep red carpet flanked by stone slabs, a light from the central chandelier that seemed brilliant after their benighted journey, and above all the excited chatter of familiar voices, asking each other how they were, telling of adventures on the way and wrong turnings taken, all infused by the relief of knowing they were safe at last. And here were Walter and Viv, the last to arrive. 'Well done, Walter! Trust you to get lost!'

Jane allowed herself to be led up the huge staircase, with such shallow steps, across the broad landing which was embellished with portraits of the ancestors of the family that owned Somerton Court, the Somertons, who traced their lineage to Henry II's time. Dick Sumpton, it was explained, had done the king a great service in France, was knighted as Sir Richard Somerton and given an old manor house that nobody else had any use for. Jane did not absorb the details but walked across the landing as if in a dream, down the corridor which led off it and into her room for the weekend.

It was a small room, with one curved wall which gave the impression of protection, evidently part of a tower at the corner of the house. The thick carpet, deep red curtains, white bed, wash-basin, cases of books and, on a small bedside table, a vase of flowers, all spoke to her of warmth and security and loving care. Jane thanked her guide who left with a cheerful, 'Supper in ten

130

minutes', sat on the bed and wept with relief and delight.

'A quick think'

Supper, in the panelled dining-room, was a delightful meal, not hurried, nor even spoilt by the request from the management that volunteers would be welcome to wash up afterwards.

Somerton Court was now managed by a charitable trust in collaboration with the present owners of the house and it was available for groups of up to thirty at a very reasonable rate, considering the luxury of the house. But it was not the plush surroundings that made the greatest impression. It was the love and care with which the visitors were welcomed, summed up for Jane in the bowl of flowers, for Diana in the en suite bathroom which made looking after Rebecca so much easier. Everyone felt that an individual effort had been made for them alone.

The evening programme was in tatters by this time, but nobody seemed to mind. Coffee in the hall by the log fire, while the first squad of washers did the dishes, provided time for a rearrangement and it was well past nine o'clock before the company was assembled in the library for their first meeting.

The visiting speakers were now formally introduced, though they appeared to be old friends to many already. Howard and Heather they wished to be called ('our surname always causes confusion') and they gave an immediate impression of understanding the Canwell Park situation. They seemed to take in the whole group as part of an extended conversation, rather than 'giving a talk'. They interrupted one another and seemed to have no script, but succeeded in conveying an impression of competence and security.

'It's much too late now for the groups we had hoped to have this evening,' Howard was saying, 'but, in your case, this really doesn't matter too much because you seem to have done so much preparatory work already in your house groups over the past three months. So we've had a quick think over supper ...'

'You mean *you* have,' put in Heather. 'You know I always agree with your rearrangements.'

'*We* have had a quick think,' pursued Howard doggedly, 'in that I always decide on a course which I know Heather will approve of. Life isn't worth living if I don't!'

'Listen to him!' said Heather. 'That's how he gets his own way. I hope you will do as we say and not as we do this weekend.'

Even Diana began to think that this couple would not lay down rules which she would have to oppose. In any case she didn't feel like opposing anyone at the moment. She and Timothy had brought Rebecca earlier in the afternoon, before the worst of the fog. Then the warmth of their welcome, the relief at seeing everyone arrive in one piece, and the evening meal, safe in the knowledge that Becky was asleep upstairs and one of the staff would let her know if there were any small cries from that quarter, had all made her serenely sleepy and comfortable.

The programme

'So what *we've* done,' said Howard, totally unmoved by

his wife's interruptions, 'is to give the six groups an agenda for tomorrow. The group leaders know who they are. If things had gone according to plan you would be meeting now to formulate your own agenda, but we've had an update from Diana and Timothy about your house groups and will leave you to form your working groups tomorrow and on Sunday.'

'The idea is,' went on Heather without a pause, or any sign between them that it was her turn to speak, 'that we have a full session in the morning in your working groups, tackling these questions. Then, after coffee, we shall do some practical work on personal relationships.' Gina looked at Bob, who made a wry face. 'Don't worry,' said Heather, seeing Bob's grimace, 'there'll be nothing very intense or embarrassing. Then we have the afternoon free, a full session together after tea to share the groups' findings and a bit of an impromptu party after supper.'

'On Sunday,' said Howard, again without a pause, 'we shall have working groups first, then a Communion service. After lunch we'll have a final sharing session and then back to suburbia.'

'But we've only just arrived,' wailed Gina. 'We can do without suburbia.'

'Perhaps we should for a while,' said Heather. 'That's what we're here for, to be in a different place. But we are not here to escape from reality. We've often said of this kind of weekend that it's not a hole in the ground for Christian ostriches to hide their heads in to escape from reality, but a hole in the clouds for Christian giraffes to poke their heads through to find Reality with a capital R. And that's our hope for this weekend – that we shall all learn to live more comfortably in the kingdom of God.'

133

They sang a few hymns and choruses, prayed together and went to bed with a feeling of joy and contentment and also of anticipation of what might emerge in the rest of the weekend.

When Gordon and Margaret reached their room Gordon opened his envelope and groaned. 'What's the matter now?' Margaret was trying the bed and finding it soft and inviting. She was in no mood for problems.

'It's just our luck, Margot,' he said. He called her Margot only when he felt the need of comfort. 'I've got the Peter and Paul group.'

'What's wrong with that?'

'The question for my group is, "How do we interpret for today Peter and Paul's instructions to wives to submit to and obey their husbands?" Then it gives the references. We're sure to upset someone, either by being too narrow-minded or too broad-minded.'

'Not everyone can see both sides of every question and agree with them both as you do,' said Margaret sweetly. 'But let's worry about that tomorrow. This bed looks very comfortable.'

'What have you got for your group?' Margaret was to lead a group of her own.

'Singleness,' she said. 'Where does singleness fit into the pattern? It doesn't appear in the Garden of Eden, except that Adam was all lonesome before Eve came along.'

'How will you cope with that?'

'I don't know, but I'm not going to worry about it now.' Margaret happily stretched herself on the bed. 'Over the past few years you have been teaching me not to worry and I think I'm learning. The group can decide what it thinks tomorrow.'

Gina and Bob, however, did not settle down so easily. 'Does John 3:16 cancel Genesis 3:16? Does the cross cancel out the fall? Are Christians in some way returned to the innocent state that mankind enjoyed in the Garden of Eden?' Gina showed Bob the paper. Their light was not turned off until late.

Meanwhile, both Nigel and Sallie had been asked to lead a discussion and they both felt it to be a promotion.

'We're among the heavies now, my dear, the "A team",' said Nigel. 'Submission and love, are they equal demands? If not, which is the harder? Wow! And I've got Mrs Beesley and Viv James in my group. What have you got?'

'"How do we get right ideas from head to heart? How can we be motivated to *do* as well as to *think* properly?" And I've got Joan and Edith in my group.' Joan Jenkins, Carol's mother, had followed her husband into a charismatic understanding of the work of God.

'What can I do? Whenever you ask Edith Kent a question she says "Jesus", and whenever you ask Joan she says "the Holy Spirit".'

'That's very unkind, Sallie, and you know it. Even so, I'd like to hear what happens.'

How important is it for a weekend conference to meet in a comfortable place?
Does it draw people nearer to God or insulate them from him?

16

Tea and hot buttered toast

Saturday dawned clear and bright. Early risers had seen fog from their windows, one or two had taken a pre-breakfast walk and arrived back with glistening hair and eyebrows, but the sky above was blue and the pale disc of the sun was already visible.

Most people were refreshed by a good night's sleep and others were warmed by the sight of the newly-lighted log fire and a truly English breakfast, including bacon and sausage and eggs and toast and marmalade... 'We never bother at home.' 'I only have cereal.' 'Toast is all I can manage.' The comments were predictable. Fortified by the rare experience of a hot meal, therefore, the groups prepared for action at nine thirty.

Peter and Paul

Gordon Barber pushed open the oaken door of The Study with a sinking feeling in his stomach. His task was daunting indeed. In rather under one and a half hours he had to take his group through the problem of how to interpret the New Testament letters on the subject of male headship and, if possible, produce an agreed report.

As if that was not problem enough, just look at the people he had in the group! Five others sat waiting for him. Bob Renshaw, always ready to stand by 'the Bible as it is with no frills attached'; Cyril Kent, newly released from his home where he had been imprisoned since his stroke and eager for the discussion (surely a close ally for Bob); Carol Jenkins, taking a weekend off from university, who did not usually agree with traditional thinking; Gavin Morrison, the only other young person there, presumably to keep Carol company, and Connie Bassett, already overfilling a huge armchair in the corner.

Gordon had decided that his best hope of keeping the peace and producing some agreement was to make a statement of agreed principles to begin with. They read the Bible extract, Ephesians 5:22-33, and Gordon began:

'We're assuming,' he said, 'that we all agree with Timothy's ground rule that what is in the Bible is there because God meant it to be there. What Paul wrote is not there by mistake ...'

'And that it's God's Word to be obeyed and acted upon, not just Paul's opinion to be debated,' said Bob, before Gordon could take a breath.

'And that Paul lived in a society very different from ours, so we need to interpret what he said against that background.' That was Carol.

'And that you shouldn't interrupt the chairman.' That was Connie.

'Thank you Connie,' said Gordon, 'but yes. I'll take both those interruptions as agreed, if you are all happy. The background of Paul's writing works two ways. In the first place it was the background of the Jewish and Greek and Roman traditions, whereby women were definitely second-class citizens. Rabbis thanked God that they were not women, soldiers wrote home to their pregnant wives saying, "if it's a girl throw it out" and women had no education, very few rights and very little dignity.

'In the second place, there had been a revolution brought about by Jesus, who had depended on the care of women, allowed them to approach him in public, showed himself first to a woman after his resurrection, in fact treated them as human beings. Jesus probably did more for the emancipation of women than anyone before or since and Paul picked this up. "In Christ there is neither male nor female ... all are one in Christ Jesus" (Galatians 3:28).

'Now let's follow the principles Timothy gave us. One: what does the Bible *say*? In this case, "Wives, submit to your husbands ... Husbands, love your wives, just as Christ loved the church and gave himself up for her." Two: what is the principle behind that? That husbands and wives have a *very* profound duty to respect and care for one another in the appropriate manner. And that because they are different their duties to each other will be different.

138

'Paul used the language of his day when he called wives to submit. Amazingly he did not tell husbands to *rule*, but to *love*. Yes, we'll have a discussion in a minute, but just let me finish first.

'Three: how do we apply that principle to our own day? "Husbands, love your wives" is easy – at least it's easy to *understand*, very difficult to do.'

'Margaret should know,' chortled Connie.

'But "wives, submit", how do we translate that?

'Submit,' said Cyril, firmly.

'Agree,' said Carol.

'Respect (Ephesians 5:33),' said Bob.

'I'll settle for "respect",' said Gordon. 'You see we must hold on to the principle that Paul is telling us something true and profound, but we must also allow for the change in society today without losing the Bible's authority. If we have to choose between modern society and the Bible's authority, then the Bible is right every time. But we can apply the principles to our own day without trying to recreate the social conditions of near-slavery that women lived in. To demand that women *submit* to their husbands today is not to apply the spirit of God's word but to recreate the society of two thousand years ago.'

There followed much discussion and, even though Cyril was reluctant, Gordon's final point was carried.

Silly jokes

For some time Gordon's group had been vaguely disturbed by the gales of laughter coming from the next room. The session, under Gina's leadership, had started seriously. The question they had to address was ponderous enough: does Jesus' death on the cross cancel the fall for those who accept his forgiveness? And, if so, does it mean that Christians are back in the blissful Garden of Eden situation?

They had agreed that Jesus came to offer new life and a new creation for those who follow him and that in one sense the curse of the fall was reversed. Disobedience has been turned to obedience in those who have repented, and forgiveness means that we are no longer under God's just condemnation.

But it was also agreed that this new life put the clock forward into eternal life, which starts now, rather than putting the clock back to mankind's original state. It was agreed furthermore that the big difference between the Garden of Eden and Canwell Park was that sin was still around in the latter. We are forgiven, but we are still sinners and cannot possibly return to the innocent state of Adam and Eve.

So the group agreed on all points in a relatively short time. It must have been the comparison between the Garden of Eden and Canwell Park that prompted the merriment, but the serious discussion was at an end. The weather was put forward as another contrast between the idyllic state and SW31 and someone mentioned clothes, or lack of them, which caused some merriment. It was thought that the bus service might have been better before the fall, but there wouldn't have been anywhere to go.

Gina tried to consider another serious question: how far should we try to have ideal relationships, such as Adam and Eve had? But this caused more merriment, the most serious contribution being 'how could we know whether to imitate their relationship when we didn't know what it was like anyway?' Gina gave up and joined in the fun.

As she did so she was sharply aware that she had failed. Her group was a riot. They were surely disturbing the groups on either side of them, even though the walls were thick. Yet had they failed? They had answered their question very quickly. There was no point in prolonging the discussion. They were enjoying themselves and there was no harm in that. And she realized something else. Diana was laughing. It was the first time that she had seen Diana looking something like her old self. Her eyes were shining and her colour was returning. The combined effects of the warm welcome and these silly remarks made by loving friends had started Diana on her road to recovery.

Gina herself had suffered much from depression and knew that the road might be long and difficult, but it looked as if the corner had been turned. Prayer, medication, counselling, all these may have played their part, but God had chosen to use a warm fire and some rather poor jokes to signal the start of healing.

In the midst of her laughter Gina gave thanks.

Long live the differences

'How did you get on this morning, then?'

Viv and Walter James were enjoying the free afternoon. The sun was shining strongly, even warmly for late November, and Somerton Court was surrounded by woodlands. Couples and small groups strolled among the trees, occasionally encountering each other and comparing notes about views they had discovered or animals or birds that they thought they had seen.

'I think Timothy was very good,' said Walter in reply to his wife's question.

'I thought it was meant to be a discussion.'

'Well it was, but he had it pretty well organized and we all agreed with him. The main point was that men ought to be men and women ought to be women and we get into all kinds of confusion if we try to pretend otherwise.'

'Sounds a bit chauvinistic.'

'No, he was absolutely ... *we* were absolutely firm on equality. Men and women have equal roles to play, but they are different roles.'

'What's the difference, then?' said Viv. 'I mean apart from having children and being physically smaller. I've heard Gordon on this and he says that there's not much scientific evidence for other differences.'

'No, not scientific, but generally perceived. He said that the basic underlying aspect of maleness is responsibility, responsibility to care for the world and each other, to initiate and take the strain. And the basic female characteristic is responsiveness, responding to a lead, not necessarily following it but reacting to it. Most men feel comfortable taking initiatives and most women feel comfortable to let it happen, and to improve on and fill out what the male has begun. Most men are good at general overall plans and most women are good at detail. They complement each other exactly and couldn't do without each other's influence.'

'H'm!' said Viv. 'Male headship by another name.'

'Yes, OK, you could call it that,' said Walter, not wanting to argue. 'Men did not begin to take the initiative as a result of the fall. Their proper headship was twisted and spoilt by it. But, and this is the point, "headship" in this sense is not a word that implies rank or value or superiority, it merely implies function. It originally meant "source", not "authority". Somebody said that it's like one of those double tram units that you find in European cities sometimes. One of them has to be in front of the other, but nobody thinks that it's *better* than the other in any way.

'But ...', said Viv, but at this point they met Nigel and Sallie who were walking briskly in the other direction.

'Tea,' said Nigel.

'And hot buttered toast,' said Sallie.

There was no further discussion that afternoon: but this was the kind of understanding that was spreading among them all. Yet it was not the discussion groups that made the biggest impact on that Saturday.

The 'personal relationship' session had consisted of a series of role-plays expressing service. Everyone had been asked to act out some form of expression of concern for someone else. This had been a remarkably powerful event. It had dawned on many that family roles and relationships were not meant to be a matter of rules or rights, but of privileges; not 'how can I defend my position?' but 'how can I help the others?' This was to have a profound effect on the events of the following day.

How far must we bring first-century customs into our obedience to timeless principles?

How can we be sure that we have separated them correctly?

Is submission a first-century or a timeless principle?

17

'What I have done for you ...'

T imothy descended the grand staircase for the third time, carrying more of the family luggage. Why ever did they always bring so *much*, even for a couple of days? There was some sense of melancholy, too. All the others had gone and there was a feeling of let-down after all the excitement. Yet, more important than this, Timothy felt a profound gratitude and relief.

It was always a relief to come to the happy end of a weekend you were responsible for. But it had been much more than happy. There had been understanding, growth in love and caring, breaking down of the barriers of mistrust and, above all for Timothy, Diana really seemed to be improving at last. The weekend had shown him something that he had really known all along, too. He could not have Sue as his curate. He must settle that very soon.

He thought back over the day. They were all feeling warm and secure after their final session of worship and prayer. It had been very quiet, even low-key, but they had sensed a powerful presence with them – several people as different as Mrs Beesley and Fred Jenkins had mentioned it.

Singles: alone but not lonely

Then there was the reporting back from the remaining groups which had met yesterday. Yesterday? It seemed like a year ago. Nigel and Sallie had both done very well. It had been a good move to get them leading groups.

Nigel had had a tough assignment. Like Gordon, he had got involved with the crucial question of how to interpret the word 'submit' in Ephesians 5. He had cheated a bit, because Gordon and Nigel had compared notes between their group meetings and the reporting back session, so they had fitted their reports around each other to make complementary points. Very helpful, though.

Gordon had already suggested that 'submit' was Paul's and Peter's word, appropriate for their society but in need of translation for ours. The Bible's underlying message was one of respect, so why not use that word instead?

Nigel's group had stopped short of this and Nigel's report had turned into a response to Gordon's. Timothy smiled as he remembered the debate.

'You can't dictate to Paul what he meant. If he wrote

"submit", that was for all of us.' Cries of support from Cyril and Bob, who had never really agreed with Gordon.

'The point is surely that, although it is extremely hard for wives to agree to submit, it is equally hard for husbands to love their wives in the self-sacrificing way that Jesus showed us. If wives and husbands were less interested in claiming their rights and their status and more interested in supporting one another, there would be no need for an argument at all. Husbands are called to submissive love and wives to loving submission.'

This point had gone down very well, especially after the morning Communion service.

Then Margaret had been a great success with her group on singleness. Even Jane Goodrich had been encouraged by it. What were the points they had made?

In the first place, marriage is not the ultimate destiny for us. Jesus taught that in heaven there will be no marriage (Luke 20:34-36). This must mean that our relationships with each other will all be better than the best marriage. 'They are God's children.' God's family in heaven is better off than any married couple here.

Then Jesus was not married, and he was surely the supreme example of a human being. Those who said that marriage or sexual relations were necessary for a person to be mature had better look at Jesus. Was anyone ever more mature than he was? In any case the Bible stressed the value of singleness as well as the value of marriage. If Adam and Eve represent mankind and womankind, Genesis 2 means that men and women are necessary for each other, not that each man needs one woman or vice versa.

That was all very well, but single people were often *lonely*. Someone had said that being alone was better than the utter loneliness of living in a bad marriage, but it was also underlined that the church ought to be an example to the world of the family of God. Single people must be often alone but should never need to be *lonely*. It was the responsibility of the church community to see to it that everyone felt part of the fellowship. The point was noted.

Head to heart

The final group had been Sallie's. She had handled it particularly well. 'How do we get our ideas from head to heart, to really *want* to do the things we know we ought to do?' At worst the group might have developed into an argument. Those, like Edith Kent, who said that the Bible gave you all the motivation you needed, said, 'If it's in God's Word, then get on with it and don't complain.' On the other hand people like Joan Jenkins were inclined to say that there's no point in trying because we always fail. 'Let go and let God' was her motto.

Sallie had managed to include both points of view in a report that was really a talk on the Trinity. The centre of it all, she had said, was the need for submission, not just of one lot of human beings to another, but of all of us to God. Once we are willing to let God be God and accept that he is real and interested in what we do, then we can take three steps:

Submit our wills to that of Christ – what we all said we did at conversion or baptism or confirmation or whatever – do it again. Then, because we can't do it on our own, open ourselves to the influence of the Holy Spirit. He alone can provide us with the motive power. Then in gratitude for all that he has done, follow God the Father's way in company with the rest of his children. 'All this should be done in great humility,' said Sallie. 'We should read Philippians chapter two. And if you don't get round to it here's an extract: "Continue to work out your salvation with fear and trembling, for it is God who works in you to will and to act according to his good purpose" (verses 12-13).'

The whole weekend, thought Timothy, had been a working out of those principles. The discussion groups had been necessary, the understanding of biblical interpretation was necessary, agreed statements were necessary, but none of them would be of any use if people's wills and feelings were not engaged. No talk about God was of any use if God himself was not really involved and allowed to take a part in the proceedings. And that is what had happened at the Communion service.

'Do this in remembrance of me'

Was it possible to analyse how that service had made such an impact? Like the final session it had been quiet, almost serene. If they had stirred up the feelings, especially of the younger folk, with a hefty session of chorus singing, would God have been more obviously present? Timothy thought not. No, the whole programme had worked together to focus on the Communion. It had not been planned that way, not by Timothy anyway. The warm and welcoming house and staff had contributed, the study the Canwell Park people had already done had helped. The Saturday morning session when they had done role-plays of service had been very influential. Everything pointed to something, but what was it to be?

The service was very informal. They sat in a circle with a simple table bearing a flagon of wine and a loaf of bread in the centre as a focus. Howard and Heather shared the Bible reading and the short address in such a way that nobody could remember afterwards what part each of them had played, but the substance of their contribution was memorable.

They read and talked about Jesus' washing his disciples' feet, John 13:1-17. It had been a momentous occasion. It was 'just before the Passover Feast' in Jerusalem and Jesus was there for the last time. John tells us that Jesus now showed his disciples the full extent of his love. This was to be demonstrated completely at the crucifixion, but already, at supper, there appeared an opportunity to symbolize that love.

It appeared that no servant was on hand to wash the feet of the guests, a customary courtesy in a hot country where travellers wore open sandals and streets were dusty. The disciples of Jesus probably wondered whether to say anything about it. Perhaps each felt that he should offer, but none took the initiative. They had all decided to make the best of it and forget the ceremony when Jesus himself took the water and towel and began to wash their feet. Peter spoke for them all as usual. 'No, Lord, you mustn't do that! I am your servant!'

The Servant King looked up at Peter and said, 'Unless I wash you, you are not on my side.'

'Oh, in that case, Lord, fine. Do me all over!'

Jesus must have smiled at Peter's exuberance, but he carefully and lovingly finished washing his feet. Peter was dimly aware that this was a complete reversal of all that he had been used to. The Lord was doing the servant's task. It needed doing, it was no mere symbolic gesture, no Maundy Thursday ceremony. To wash another's feet it is necessary to bow before them, to bend in appreciation of their dignity. The Lord had become the servant. To become true servants the disciples had to accept service.

It was at this point that Gina suddenly realized that she needed to accept Bob's care for her, even if it was mistaken in its expression. And it was at this point that Bob realized that service to be real, loving service, has to be what the person needs and wants, not what the server arrogantly prescribes. Their hands touched in mutual understanding.

'I am your Teacher and your Lord,' said Jesus. 'Quite so. And what I have done for you, you should be doing for one another.'

What was the equivalent of foot-washing that each person present could do for the others? Edith remembered very vividly that she had literally washed Cyril's feet after his stroke. Sallie silently thanked Nigel for the housework he did. Bob was deciding to ask Gina whether she wanted to go somewhere else on a Thursday or stay at home together. Gina was deciding to ask if she could play dominoes. All round the circle people were using their imagination and being determined to serve one another.

'Then the Lord who had washed his followers' feet turned to the place of execution and went purposefully to death for the benefit of those followers.' This very wine they were drinking together and the bread they were breaking for each other were the potent memorials of that blood and broken body. The Lord who had washed their feet in water was offering to wash their very selves in his blood.

This was the true meaning of all relationships, man and woman included, 'do this in remembrance of me.' Do what? Eat and drink, yes, and live and love and serve one another. 'As I have loved you, so you should love one another.'

Between the Communion service and lunch there was a space of half an hour. No-one was surprised that there was complete silence, because for once no-one had anything to say.

Do you think that Margaret's group did justice to the 'singles' (unmarried mothers, widows, widowers, divorcees as well as 'traditionally' single people)? What more is needed? Will you do it?
How does the cross make sense of all human relationships as you see it?

18

The Adam and Eve agenda

So the Canwell Park story continues, an 'everyday story of suburban folk', but where does that leave our understanding of the whole issue? Many ideas have been voiced, but which of them are we supposed to agree with? Is it possible to discover the right way through the maze of controversy about submission? We can at least see the whole matter in an orderly perspective and then make up our own minds.

Headship in the Garden?

Timothy Monteith called the basic will of God for man/woman relationship 'factor x'. I prefer the phrase 'the

Adam and Eve agenda'. This is how God planned it in the first place – the ideal, perfect relationship. The problem is that we are not told in Genesis what this was. It's just round the corner: out of our sight. We have clues: Adam and Eve were made in God's image; Adam came first but Eve was necessary to complete him; they were equal, but very different from each other...

If there was headship in the Garden of Eden (that is, if God's perfect plan intended headship of one over the other), we can only infer what it was like by studying the twisted, fallen nature of it that we find in Genesis 3, in history and in life about us now. We shall return to this presently.

Emergency order or God's plan?

Whatever the perfect plan for relationship was it was radically changed by the rebellion of mankind, called the fall. Eve and then Adam disobeyed God's only negative command, ate the fruit and died to the ideal life God had envisaged.

Man immediately took on a domineering, arrogant stance; woman rebelled and alternately fawned and fought back. Thank God that this is not the whole picture, but it expresses the groundswell of male/female relationships (Genesis 3:16). This is an appalling situation and needs to be remedied, but how?

If we believe that the Adam and Eve agenda gives us male headship, then we shall have to work towards restoring proper, loving and appropriate headship in place of the twisted, arrogant version we now see. But if we believe that the agenda means total equality in every area, we have to assume that male headship is an emergency order, tolerated by God in the light of mankind's disobedience, but to be fought against and eliminated if possible. So some Christians will work towards the abolition of male headship, others towards its perfection. Toleration and understanding are needed here.

The new creation

Man/woman relationships took a sharp turn with the life, death and resurrection of Jesus. In the first place he went out of his way to accord women an honoured place in society, which they had almost entirely lost. This was no condescending gesture, like the all-men's club arranging a Ladies' Evening ('the ladies, God bless them!'). No, Jesus treated women as people on the level with men, talked to them in public, valued their care and fellowship and signalled to the world that God, at least, did not regard them as in any way inferior to men, but different in function and approach. Thus he did not appoint women among his twelve storm-troopers for the kingdom, but he did reveal himself first after the resurrection to a woman. (Women's testimony was not, in those days, acceptable in a court of law.)

The good news of the New Testament is that the cross and resurrection, followed by the coming of the Holy Spirit, produce a new environment for mankind, a new creation of relationships. God forgives those who accept Christ and adopts them into his family. We are commanded then to love and forgive each other. A new order is possible.

Does this mean the reversal of the fall? Yes, in that male domination and female rebellion can be conquered. No, in that the tendency in those directions remains with us and needs to be fought.

Can we then return to the Adam and Eve agenda, supposing that we agree what it was? We shall never reach that degree of perfection this side of heaven but, yes, we should aim for it. So what is it we're aiming for? We're back where we started, not knowing whether we're aiming for headship or equality.

Peter, Paul and submission

It's at this point that the debate over Paul and Peter, the New Testament letters' stand on submission, can be a help to us. Wives are called to submit to their husbands. Women are expected to keep silent in church. If we have any respect at all for the authority of the Bible as God's communication to mankind, we cannot discard this as cultural lumber. It must be taken seriously. But it must be culturally understood.

Paul and Peter were expressing the Adam and Eve agenda in terms appropriate to their time. And Paul particularly added the real dynamite when he told husbands to love and respect their wives sacrificially. Everyone knew wives ought to obey their husbands, but here was something revolutionary. What? Husbands had duties too?

These letter-writers-extraordinary were telling us something we need to know about the Adam and Eve agenda. Men and women need to respond to each other appropriately but not identically. There are duties both ways, as well as delights, but who is to say which comes off best? The answer is, of course, that in complementarity both come off best if they can work out proper

155

submission-love and responsible-love towards each other.

'The church sank ...'

We really seem to be getting somewhere now, but unfortunately two thousand years of history have stirred up the mud again. We approach the Bible's revelation wearing spectacles smudged, stained and muddied by what we have been brought up to believe, *our* cultural inheritance that is, and by theories which are flying about our heads in the media.

The church quickly sank from the high point of New Testament ideals and women became alternately suppressed, used and abused, and praised, idolized and pampered. The gallant male managed to keep the female in subservience and at the same time condescend graciously to her being 'the weaker sex'. Women varied between accepting these flatteries, bowing to the inevitable 'weaker' image and infiltrating male-dominated society as abbesses, merchants and nobles (with the occasional queen thrown in) and later hospital matrons, reformers and missionaries, company bosses and prime ministers.

But our cultural heritage, emphasized by our male-dominated vocabulary so hated by the feminists (*man*-kind, chair*man*, lay*man* and so on), tells us that men are the bosses: women the second-raters.

This is the backcloth for the emancipation movements of the past couple of centuries, suffragettes and the new feminism. This has thrown new clouds of dust into our eyes, because we are told by the media that women and men must be equal in every way and some would desire us to be *uniform*, in dress, manner, employment and so on. Some genuinely aim for female domination to balance the male domination of the past.

There is a massive jargon-emphasis today on *rights* rather than *duties*. Women have a right to their bodies (translated, this means freedom to have sex with whom they please without being tied to a husband and the choice of abortion on demand). Self-fulfilment and the right to happiness are the dominant self-evident 'truths' of our society. Where, then, does the simple Christian find a place for duties and responsibilities? These are old-hat and are to be jettisoned, it seems.

No wonder we are in a muddle about male/female relationships. Christians, just like everyone else, are steeped in current notions. In this debate, as in the riot at Ephesus, described in Acts 19, 'the assembly was in confusion. Some were shouting one thing, some another. Most of the people did not even know why they were there.'

Agenda for action

Six suggestions, then, to help us to come to our own conclusion as to what the Adam and Eve agenda must be:

1. *Try to understand the biblical principles properly*.
Do your level best to slice through the encrusted prejudices of the past 2000 years and the pompous hot air of the contemporary media and evaluate reverently and carefully what the overall message of the Bible is.

157

2. *Try to understand one another.*

Use your imagination about where the other person 'is coming from'. Perhaps women do think and feel rather differently from men, but avoid like the plague the idea that women feel and men think. Allow a wide margin for misunderstanding and try very hard not to decide the end of a discussion before it has begun. Also try to avoid generalizing about men and women. We are all people and people are unique individuals.

3. *Keep communication going.*

Do not allow silence to stifle dialogue. Remember that you are both on the same side, looking for truth and not occupying defensive positions which need to be invested. If you do find that happening, ask seriously whether it is a matter of principle you are defending or perhaps some insecurity you are compensating for.

4. *Pray together if possible.*

Worship together in the company of others even if you find prayer face to face too difficult. Acknowledgment of God's presence in the relationship breaks down 'we two' into 'we three', which is much more healthy.

5. *Ask for help.*

Don't hesitate to bring in some third party who can be trusted, in confidence. Do not share your problems openly with all and sundry, which is gossip, but be humble enough to ask for counselling. This is a victory, not a defeat. And attend conferences and retreats, which will often have beneficial effects.

6. *Allow your ideas to make the 18-inch journey from head to heart.*

The difference between 'I ought' and 'I want' is often the difference between something not happening and actually coming to fruition. This is a mysterious business: how does it happen? Can I make myself want what I ought to want? The answer is probably no. The wind blows where it chooses. The Holy Spirit of God works where he can and where he will. If we are open to him, change is on the menu.

With these six suggestions in mind you might like to read this book again, and pick up clues as you go along.

Finale

Meanwhile, Gordon and Margaret Barber were driving home from Somerton Court. The car was full of light-hearted conversation. Jane, especially, seemed happier than Margaret had ever known her to be and Gina and Bob seemed very easy together. Gone was the freezing fog of the outward journey and they drove quietly back in the light of the November afternoon.

Their passengers were returned to their respective homes in Fairview Avenue and Gordon and Margaret turned thankfully for home. Margaret's sister had been staying for the weekend to 'look after' Shelley, but it appeared that Jason had been doing his share of caring, for both he and Shelley were unsteadily progressing down the footpath on roller skates. When she saw her parents, Shelley grabbed Jason by the arm and they stood, almost still, waiting for the car to draw up.

Before they could open the door Shelley shrieked at the top of her voice, 'I've asked Jason to marry me and he said yes, didn't you Jason?'

Jason, as usual, said nothing.

'Good grief!' said Gordon.